W9-BHZ-742

Painted Whimsies

Decorative Accents
for the
Home and Garden

JENNIFER R. FERGUSON
AND
JUDITH A. SKINNER

Martingale™
& COMPANY

Painted Whimsies:
Decorative Accents for the
Home and Garden

© 2002 by Jennifer R. Ferguson
and Judith A. Skinner

Martingale & Company
20205 144th Avenue NE
Woodinville, WA 98072-8478
www.martingale-pub.com

President ~ Nancy J. Martin
CEO ~ Daniel J. Martin
Publisher ~ Jane Hamada
Editorial Director ~ Mary V. Green
Managing Editor ~ Tina Cook
Technical Editor ~ Chris Rich
Copy Editor ~ Liz McGehee
Design Director ~ Stan Green
Photographer ~ Brent Kane
Cover and Text Designer ~ Stan Green

Mission Statement

We are dedicated to providing quality products and service by working together to inspire creativity and to enrich the lives we touch.

No part of this product may be reproduced in any form, unless otherwise stated, in which case reproduction is limited to the use of the purchaser. The written instructions, photographs, designs, projects, and patterns are intended for the personal, noncommercial use of the retail purchaser and are under federal copyright laws; they are not to be reproduced by any electronic, mechanical, or other means, including informational storage or retrieval systems, for commercial use. Permission is granted to photocopy patterns for the personal use of the retail purchaser.

The information in this book is presented in good faith, but no warranty is given nor results guaranteed. Since Martingale & Company has no control over choice of materials or procedures, the company assumes no responsibility for the use of this information.

Printed in China
07 06 05 04 03 02   8 7 6 5 4 3 2 1

Library of Congress Cataloging-in-Publication Data

Ferguson, Jennifer R.
    Painted whimsies : decorative accents for the home and garden/
Jennifer R. Ferguson and Judith A. Skinner.
        p. cm.
    ISBN 1-56477-451-1
  1. Painting. 2. Decoration and ornament. 3. House furnishings.
4. Garden ornaments and furniture. I. Skinner, Judith A. II. Title.

    TT385 .F47 2002
    745.7'23—dc21

                                                            2002011260

Dedication

Jennifer dedicates *Painted Whimsies* to her children, Ashley and Tyler, with these words: What a blessing from God you both are. I'm so lucky to have two incredible kids who bring such joy to my life. Watching you grow is the greatest of gifts. I thank you for your love and understanding, and for the sacrifices you made during the time that I spent creating this book. I love you with all my heart and more than words can express.

Judy dedicates *Painted Whimsies* to her grandchildren, Joshua Hugh and Samantha Rea, with these words: You are more precious than life itself. I hope that I can help you both achieve your dreams and goals in life, as I've achieved mine. You both make me proud to be a grandma.

Acknowledgments

We would like to express our immense gratitude to the people who helped create this book:

Martingale & Company, for publishing *Painted Whimsies*; Mary Green, Donna Lever, and Terry Martin, for their continued support and for answering all of our quirky little questions; Jay and Mary Jones, for their endless support and for making all of our wooden projects; DecoArt, for supplying us once again with their wonderful Americana Acrylic paint and other products; Eagle Brush Company, for supplying all of our artist's brushes; Chris Rich, for doing a wonderful editing job again; Brent Kane, for being incredible! (What else can we say?)

And finally, our families (Jennifer's husband, Jim, and their children, Ashley and Tyler; and Judy's husband, Don, their children, and their family members Donnie, Renee, Joshua, Shanel, Ciera, Rex, Joanie, Corrie, Bob, and Samantha), not only for believing in us, but also for putting up with all that it takes to create a book.

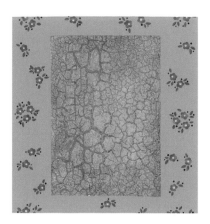  

CONTENTS

Introduction

In recent years, the popularity of stenciled and faux-painted walls and furniture has soared. While painting your house and furniture may be a wonderful way to brighten up your life, if you've never held a brush before, the easiest and most satisfying way to learn the arts of stenciling and faux painting is to start by painting small household objects. *Painted Whimsies* will show you how. And once you've learned the basics, you'll probably want to paint everything in sight, including those walls and dining room chairs.

Does your basement or attic harbor an old file cabinet that's too scratched to display? Are your houseplants pining away in plain terra-cotta pots with no pizzazz? Is your metal mailbox so mundane that the postman can barely find it? If so, *Painted Whimsies* is the book for you. With its help, you'll soon be on your way to creating a file cabinet so colorful that organizing your office will feel like going to a party. Or you'll be stenciling a mailbox that's guaranteed to catch the eye of every passer-by, or painting flowerpots to perk up every plant in the house. A world of stunning projects awaits you within these pages, from gorgeous garbage cans and decorated lap desks to canisters, stepping-stones, and more.

Many of the everyday items that we've chosen as projects for this book can be used in creative ways. Why, for example, should a painted bucket live its entire life as a bucket? Why not use it to store kindling for your fireplace, folded hand towels, magazines, or toys? Flower-pots and saucers can be reborn as birdbaths, bird feeders, or even gumball holders; and a wooden box can find new life as a beautiful utensil holder. We have offered suggestions for ways to use your painted projects, but we're sure that if you let your imagination run free, you'll discover even more.

Getting started is easy; we'll guide you through every step. First, you'll learn about the tools and supplies that you'll need. Then we'll teach you how to prepare different surfaces for painting. Next, you'll explore the world of decorative painting techniques; we've explained each one in detail. Finally, you'll learn how to personalize your projects and protect their painted surfaces. Once you've browsed through these sections of *Painted Whimsies*, you'll be ready to choose a project and begin. We hope, of course, that your first project will inspire you to create many more.

Every project featured in this book comes with step-by-step instructions that will guide you from start to finish. To help you achieve professional results, we've named the specific colors and stencils that we used to paint each project. Of course, you may want to combine painting techniques, designs, and colors from several different projects to create a uniquely decorated item of your own.

—*Jennifer R. Ferguson*

—*Judith A. Skinner*

Tools and Supplies

In this section, we've provided two lists of the tools and supplies that we've used to prepare and paint the projects in this book. The first list, "Required Tools and Supplies," includes the standard items and products that you must have on hand no matter which project you choose to create, so gather them all before you start painting.

To make some of the projects, you'll also need a few special items and products; these are described in the second list, "Technique-Specific Tools and Supplies." This list may strike you as long, but don't worry. You won't need everything we've described in it unless you plan to make every project in this book! For example, to create the "All Cracked Up"

file cabinet shown on page 42, you'll need faux glazing medium, but you won't need this medium to stencil the "Apple Pickin'" pail shown on page 25. Deciding what you *will* need is easy. Each project comes with its own "Tools and Supplies" list, which includes all the technique-specific items and products required to complete it.

Required Tools and Supplies

You'll need all of the items and products described in this list, no matter which project you choose to create. Many can be found at your local home-improvement store. Others are available from crafts and art-supply stores or from mail-order suppliers. (See "Suppliers" on page 95.)

Drop Cloth or Newspapers

As you work on your project, protect your work surface with a drop cloth or several layers of newspaper.

Tack Cloth or Lint-Free Rags

After sanding a project, you'll use a tack cloth or lint-free rag to wipe away the dust that remains. Rags will also come in handy for wiping up any spilled paint.

Artist's Brushes and Stencil Brushes

An assortment of flat, round, and angle-tipped artist's brushes, from ¼" to 1" wide, is indispensable. You'll use these brushes, which yield smoother finishes than ordinary paintbrushes, to apply sealers and primers, and for some decorative painting techniques. They're available at art and crafts stores and from mail-order suppliers. You will also need stencil brushes. See page 10.

Precut Stencils

Precut stencils are sheets of plastic, each with a pattern of holes (or windows) in it. You'll add design motifs to your projects by applying paint through these windows. Stencils usually come in plastic bags. Save the bags if you can; they'll help protect your stencils when you're not using them.

Removable Painter's Tape and a Burnisher

To help affix stencils to your projects and to mask off areas that you don't want to paint, removable painter's tape (also known as "blue tape") works well. To burnish, or press down, the edges of the tape, use a burnishing tool or the edge of a plastic card, such as a credit card.

Acrylic Artist's Paints

You'll use these paints, which are available in two-ounce bottles, for all your decorative painting. For most projects, one two-ounce bottle of each color will do. (The list of acrylic paints that comes with each set of project instructions will let you know if you need more.) All the acrylic paints we've used on the projects in this book are DecoArt Americana Acrylics. (See "Suppliers" on page 95.) Please note that acrylic colors are darker when they're dry than they are in their bottles. To test a color, brush some of the paint onto a piece of paper and let it dry.

Extender

Extender, which comes in two-ounce bottles, extends the drying time of acrylic paints. Adding a drop or two to each color you use when you're stenciling will make the paint more manageable and will help create smooth finished surfaces.

Paint Palette

You'll never dip a brush directly into a bottle of paint. Instead, you'll pick up the paint from a palette. A disposable artist's palette works best for this purpose, but disposable plastic plates make good substitutes.

Wet Bags

When you stencil a project, you must start out with stencil brushes that are completely dry. You'll use one brush for each color, and as you switch back and forth between brushes, you'll place the paint-loaded brushes that you're not using into a "wet bag" so that the paint on them won't dry out before you need to use them again. To make a wet bag, just moisten a paper towel, squeeze out the excess water, and place the damp towel in a plastic bag. As you work, keep your paint-dampened stencil brushes in the wet bag, with their bristles resting on the paper towel.

Choosing Brushes

Your painting will always be at its best if you choose the right brush for the job. Below are descriptions of the artist's and stencil brushes we used to create the projects in this book.

Flats

These flat brushes, with their squared-off bristles, are ideal for base-coat painting, blocking in large areas of color, and varnishing.

Angular Flats

The bristles of these flat brushes are trimmed at an angle, so they're great for applying colors in tight corners and for painting one color next to another.

Long Liners

Also called No. 1 liners or script liner brushes, these brushes have very long bristles that come to a sharp point. They're your best choices for

painting fine lines, such as blades of grass. (See the projects on pages 55 and 83.)

Extreme Angular

When you're cutting one color in next to another color, or when you're painting the spindle areas on posts, finials, or British knobs, an extreme angular brush will work best.

Stencil Brushes

You'll need several stencil brushes, ranging from ¼" to 1" in width. Unlike artist's brushes, stencil brushes have stiff bristles and blunt ends.

Paper Towels

You'll use folded paper towels to remove excess paint from stencil brushes and, when you're creating sponged faux finishes, from your natural sea wool sponge. This paint-removal process is known as "off-loading." You'll also need paper towels for your wet bags.

Cotton Swabs

Cotton swabs work well for fixing small painting mistakes. While the paint is still wet, moisten a swab and use it to wipe away any unwanted paint. These swabs are also great for supporting wooden ball knobs and British knobs as you paint them and as the paint dries on them. (See "Preparing Wood" on pages 16–17.)

Paint Pen

For signing your finished masterpiece, a fine-tipped black paint pen is convenient and easy to handle.

Varnishes

To protect your finished project, you'll apply several coats of water-based varnish to it. Use an interior varnish for projects that will remain indoors and an exterior varnish for projects that you plan to set outdoors. Although ordinary exterior varnishes work well on projects that will simply sit outdoors, projects that will hold water, such as the "Bottoms Up" birdbath

shown on page 60, require a water-resistant exterior varnish—one that's made to withstand continuous exposure to moisture. Marine varnishes work well for this purpose. *Here's a tip:* If you plan to use a varnished container for serving food, make sure that the varnish is safe for this purpose. The manufacturer's instructions should include a warning if the varnish is toxic.

Scrubber Sponge and AC's Acrylic Craft Paint Remover

AC's Acrylic Craft Paint Remover is a solution designed to remove acrylic paints from stencils and is available from mail-order suppliers. (See "Suppliers" on page 95.) You'll use this product—and a kitchen sponge with one rough surface—to help remove paint from stencils.

Brush Cleaner/Conditioner and Brush Scrubber

To clean your stencil brushes, use a brush cleaner/conditioner and a brush scrubber. The cleaner/conditioner also works with artist's brushes. Brush scrubbers are small plastic implements with thin teeth that help remove paint from stencil-brush bristles. You can order both these items from mail-order suppliers. (See "Suppliers" on page 95.)

Artist's Water Basin

An artist's water basin will serve as a brush holder and as a rinsing basin for your artist's brushes.

Technique-Specific Tools and Supplies

To find out which of the following products and items you'll need, just refer to the "Tools and Supplies" list that accompanies the project you've selected.

Adhesive Remover

If the item that you want to paint has a sticker that won't come off, you'll need to remove the sticker with an adhesive remover. We recommend Goof Off adhesive remover. You'll find this product at home-improvement stores.

Screwdrivers

An assortment of straight-bladed and Phillips-head screwdrivers in different sizes will come in handy when you need to add hardware to a project or remove and replace existing hardware.

White Distilled Vinegar

A solution of one-half water and one-half white distilled vinegar will help remove oil and dirt from metal, glass, and tile projects before painting.

Sandpaper and Sanding Pads

Purchase sheets of sandpaper or sanding pads in several different grits or degrees of "roughness," from fine to medium. (Sanding pads are oval or round pads that function just like sandpaper; they also come in different grits.) You'll need these to prepare metal, wood, terra-cotta, and ceramic-tile surfaces before you paint them. You won't need to sand the surfaces of glass projects, but you may want to use sandpaper to smooth the coats of paint that you apply to them and to other projects.

Respirator or Dust Mask

Whenever you're sanding, work in a well-ventilated area (preferably outdoors) and wear a respirator or dust mask. Inhaling the airborne particles created during sanding isn't good for your health.

Wood Putty

If your project is wood and has any cracks, dents, or holes, you'll need to fill them with wood putty.

Water-Based Wood Sealer

Applied to unfinished wood, a coat of water-based wood sealer helps prevent warping. Several coats of sealer applied to any knots in the wood will help prevent the knots from bleeding pitch into the primer and finishes you apply over them.

Primer

Metal, wood, terra-cotta, and tile surfaces must be primed before they're painted. Primers help to seal the surface material and also help subsequent layers of paint to bond properly. Individual water-based primers for each of these four materials are available at home-improvement stores.

Gesso

Gesso is a very thick, water-based artist's primer that yields an opaque, smooth finish. You'll brush it onto your projects before you apply the base coats, and you'll also need this special primer when you use the painting technique known as "whiting out." (See "Whiting Out" on page 20.)

Watercolor Pencils

Watercolor pencils are ideal for marking off painting areas, such as the borders on the "All Cracked Up" file cabinet. (See pages 42–45.) Use light-colored pencils so the watercolor lines won't show through the paint that covers them.

Transparent Graph Ruler

You'll use a 2"-wide, 18"-long graph ruler and a watercolor pencil when you need to mark off areas that you want to paint with different base-coat colors. Because you can see through the ruler, it's especially useful when you're trying to align one marked line with another.

Empty Bottles with Lids

For some projects, you'll need an empty bottle in which to mix two different colors of paint. Empty two-ounce acrylic paint bottles work well for small amounts of paint. For larger amounts, any clean plastic or glass container with a lid will do.

Foam Brushes and Chip Brushes

The solid, wedge-shaped heads of foam brushes work well for the smooth application of glazes. Chip brushes, with their tough, stiff bristles, are wonderful for scrubbing glazes into the surface of a project or over a crackle finish. Both types of brushes are available at home-improvement stores and are so inexpensive that we treat them as "throwaways."

Natural Sea Wool Sponges

To apply sponged faux finishes, you'll need one or more natural sea wool sponges. These are available from crafts stores and are much softer than ordinary sea sponges.

Miracle Sponge and Scissors

Miracle Sponges, available at many crafts and home-improvement stores, are flat cellulose sponges that expand when they're moistened. To make the checkerboard patterns on some of the projects in this book, you'll cut square shapes from a Miracle Sponge and use the squares as paint applicators.

Cheesecloth

Wadded-up pieces of cheesecloth make good applicators for several different mediums. The textured cloth creates a distressed, variegated finish.

Gloves

When using a natural sea wool sponge or piece of cheesecloth to apply glazes, protect your hands by wearing gloves. You won't need these when you apply acrylic paints, but glazes can be quite messy.

Glass-Etching Medium, Con-Tact Paper, and an X-Acto Blade

If you make the etched window shown on page 94, you'll need a glass-etching medium to etch the permanent designs in the glass. We recommend Etchall Etching Creme, which is available from many crafts stores and mail-order suppliers. (See "Suppliers" on page 95.) You'll also need Con-Tact paper, a pencil, and an X-Acto blade for this project.

Faux Glazing Medium

You'll add this medium to acrylic paints when you want to create a sponged finish, and you'll mix it with gel stain when you want to create a negative glazed finish. The pigment-free medium, available in eight-ounce (and larger) bottles, adds translucency to painted finishes. You'll also use faux glazing medium for the "tissue-paper technique." (See the glass projects on pages 83, 85, and 87 and "Suppliers" on page 95.)

White Tissue Paper

The tissue-paper technique that we use requires covering glass surfaces with white tissue paper and faux glazing medium before you begin painting. (See the glass projects on pages 83, 85, and 87.)

Gel Stain

You'll brush these translucent stains over painted and varnished surfaces and then wipe them to give your project an antique, distressed appearance. You'll also mix gel stain with faux glazing medium to create a negative glazed finish. (See "Negative Glazed Finishes" on page 22.)

Gel stains are available in two-ounce bottles. Judy and I use DecoArt Americana Gel Stain (DS30).

Crackle Size and Venetian Plaster

These products are used to create a crackle effect. (See "Suppliers" on page 95.) You'll apply the crackle size to all the areas you wish to crackle and allow it to dry to a firm tack. Then you'll apply Venetian plaster (a "marble plaster" that's available in many different colors) over the size. One quart of each product will be more than enough to complete a single project.

One-Quart Mixing Tub and Stirring Sticks

A one-quart mixing tub and a few plastic or wooden stirring sticks will come in handy when you need to mix glazes. Both the tub and sticks are available at home-improvement stores.

Embossing Tool

To create La De Da Dots (see pages 22–23), you'll use one end of an embossing tool. This crafter's tool, which is usually used to emboss paper, is simply a stick with a small, hard metal ball at one or both ends.

Wooden Ball Knobs

A wooden ball knob is a round ball with one flat surface and a hole running partway into its center. We attach these knobs to many projects to serve as feet. They come in several different sizes and are available from crafts stores or from mail-order suppliers. (See "Suppliers" on page 95.)

Rigid Foam Block or Egg Carton

Rigid foam blocks and egg cartons can be used to help support wooden ball knobs as the paint on them dries. (See "Preparing Wood" on pages 16–17.)

E6000 Industrial Strength Adhesive

You'll need this adhesive, which is available at many crafts stores, to attach wooden ball knobs and other items to several projects. Make sure you follow the manufacturer's instructions when you use this product.

Accessories

Several of the projects in this book require accessories. These include decorative drawer pulls, a wooden finial, turned wooden beehives, British knobs, metal handles, metal rods, aluminum window-screen material, a metal door faceplate, and a metal chicken feeder that's designed to twist onto the top of a glass canning jar. Most of these items are available at home-improvement and crafts stores; the others can be ordered from mail-order suppliers.

Wood—and a Friendly Woodworker

To make the two mailboxes shown on pages 35 and 39 and the "Whimsy Critters" garden ornaments shown on page 80, you'll need a bit of wood and some woodworking experience. You will need to cut the wooden critters to size and drill holes in them, and in the case of the mailboxes, cut wooden bases and attach the posts and mailboxes to them. If you lack experience in this area, you may want to enlist the help of a friendly local woodworker.

Woodworking Tools

For a few of the projects, you'll need to drill holes, insert screws, cut wood to size, and/or attach window-screen material. Unless you prefer to have a woodworker do these jobs for you, you'll need a tape measure, an electric drill, an assortment of drill bits, a jigsaw or coping saw, a screwdriver, and a staple gun.

Surface Preparation

Before you paint your project—whether it's metal, wood, terracotta, or glass—you must prepare the surface, or the paint you apply won't adhere properly. *Here's a tip:* Once you've cleaned a project surface, try to keep your hands off it! The oil from your skin can prevent paint and other products from adhering properly.

Preparing Metal

To prepare a metal project, first use an adhesive remover to remove any stubborn stickers. (Refer to the manufacturer's instructions for the correct application technique.) Then mix a solution of one-half white distilled vinegar and one-half water. Using this solution and a scrubber sponge, wash the metal to remove all grease, oil, and dirt. Allow the metal to dry completely.

Primer will adhere to a roughened surface much better than it will to a smooth one, so the next step is to sand the metal surface lightly, using fine- to medium-grit sandpaper to dull its original finish. Use a light touch when you sand metal; you want to give the surface a bit of tooth without scratching it. If possible, do your sanding outdoors; you'll generate dust as you work. When you're done, use a lint-free rag or tack cloth to wipe away all the dust.

Next, prime the metal by using a 1"-wide artist's brush to apply several thin, even coats of water-based primer. Allow each coat to dry thoroughly before applying the next. If necessary, smooth each coat by sanding it very lightly with fine-grit sandpaper. Now you must apply several coats of gesso on top of the primer—as many coats as necessary to achieve coverage that is smooth and opaque. Use an artist's brush to apply each coat, and keep your strokes going in the same direction. Allow each coat to dry; then sand it lightly with your finest-grit sandpaper. Wipe the surface before applying the next coat.

Preparing Terra-Cotta

Remove any stickers on your terra-cotta by using an adhesive remover. Then, using fine-grit sandpaper, lightly sand any rough edges and the area where you removed the sticker. Remove the dust with a tack cloth or lint-free rag. Clean the entire surface by wiping it with a damp rag and allow the project to dry completely.

Using a 1"-wide artist's brush, prime the terra-cotta by applying several thin, even coats of water-based primer to all the areas you plan to paint. Allow each coat to dry thoroughly before applying the next. If necessary, smooth each coat by sanding it very lightly with fine-grit sandpaper. Now you must apply several coats of gesso on top of the primer—as many coats as necessary to achieve coverage that is smooth and opaque. Use an artist's brush to apply each coat, and keep your strokes going in the same direction. Allow each coat to dry; then sand it lightly with your finest-grit sandpaper. Wipe the surface before applying the next coat.

Preparing Wood

If you'd like to paint a wooden object that already has a finish on it, sand the surface well to remove any loose particles

of the existing finish and to roughen the surface of any finish that remains. New paint won't adhere to a slick finished surface. Wipe off the dust with a tack cloth or lint-free rag.

Next, if your wooden project has dents, cracks, or nail holes in it, fill them with wood putty and allow the putty to dry. Then, using a medium-grit sandpaper first and a fine-grit paper to finish up, sand the project to remove rough edges and smooth all surfaces. Always sand in the same direction as the wood grain. Wipe off the dust with a tack cloth or lint-free rag.

If the wood is unfinished, seal the entire surface by using a 1"-wide artist's brush to apply a thin, even coat of water-based wood sealer. The sealer will help prevent warping and will also raise the wood grain slightly, which in turn will help your primer and paint adhere well. Allow the sealer to dry, sand it very lightly with fine-grit sandpaper, and wipe away the dust with a rag. (To prevent any knots from bleeding pitch through the painted finishes, apply several coats of sealer over each knot, drying and sanding lightly between applications.)

Next, prime the entire project by using a 1"-wide artist's brush to apply several thin, even coats of primer,

allowing each coat to dry thoroughly before applying the next. Now you must apply several coats of gesso on top of the primer—as many coats as necessary to achieve coverage that is smooth and opaque. Use an artist's brush to apply each coat, and keep your strokes going in the same direction. Allow each coat to dry; then sand it lightly with your finest-grit sandpaper. Wipe the surface before applying the next coat.

Here's a tip: Before sealing and priming a wooden ball knob or any of the wooden accessories used in this book, insert one end of a cotton swab into the hole in the knob. Then, as you paint, hold the free end of the swab in one hand so that you won't touch the knob itself—or smear the paint on it. When

Prepare wooden knobs using a cotton swab as a handle.

you've finished painting the knob, stick the free end of the swab into a rigid foam block or an empty egg carton. The swab will hold the knob upright and prevent it from touching anything as the paint dries.

Preparing Glass and Tile

To prepare a tile surface, first sand it, using fine- to medium-grit sandpaper. (Glass surfaces don't require sanding.) If possible, do your sanding outdoors; you'll generate dust as you work. When you're

finished, use a lint-free rag or tack cloth to wipe away all the dust.

Mix a solution of one-half white distilled vinegar and one-half water. Using this solution and a scrubber sponge, wash the glass or tile to remove any grease, oil, or dirt. Allow the surface to dry completely.

Using a 1"-wide artist's brush, prime tile by applying several thin, even coats of primer to all areas you plan to paint. Allow each coat to dry thoroughly before applying the next. If necessary, smooth each coat by sanding it very

lightly with fine-grit sandpaper. Now you must apply several coats of gesso on top of the primer—as many coats as necessary to achieve coverage that is smooth and opaque. Use an artist's brush to apply each coat, and keep your strokes going in the same direction. Allow each coat to dry; then sand it lightly with your finest-grit sandpaper. Wipe the surface before applying the next coat.

For additional preparation instructions, refer to the step-by-step instructions that accompany your selected glass or tile project.

Base-Coat Painting

Once you've finished preparing your project, you'll be ready for base-coat painting—the foundation of all decorative painting effects. Each set of project instructions specifies which base-coat colors to use and where to apply them.

Pour a little paint onto a paint palette and work some of it into a flat artist's brush. Brush the paint onto the project, always stroking in the same direction. If the paint won't brush on smoothly, dip your brush into water to moisten it slightly before working the paint into the bristles.

Allow the first coat of paint to dry. If its surface is rough, use your finest-grit sandpaper to smooth it, but be careful to remove as little paint as possible. Wipe away any dust. Apply as many coats as necessary to achieve smooth, opaque coverage, letting each coat dry before applying the next.

Decorative Painting Techniques

In this section, you'll find complete instructions for all the decorative painting techniques we've used to decorate the projects in this book. You certainly don't need to memorize every detail; just turn back to these pages whenever you need to refresh your memory.

Stenciling

Stenciling is a remarkably easy painting technique, but if you've never tried it before, practice on paper. Each set of project instructions specifies which stencils to use and which colors to apply. For all the projects in this book, we've used stencils from The Stencilled Garden. These are available at specialty stencil shops and from mail-order suppliers. (See "Suppliers" on page 95.)

Positioning the Stencil

Position your stencil by locating its open design portions over the areas where you'd like the painted designs to appear. Then tape the outer edges of the stencil to the project with removable painter's tape, and burnish the tape edges well.

Positioning the Stencil

Loading and Off-Loading the Stencil Brush

Pour a little paint onto a paint palette, add one to two drops of extender, and use the handle end of your stencil brush to mix in the extender well. Next, holding your stencil brush straight up, pick up a small amount of paint with the tips of the brush bristles. Then work the paint into the bristles by swirling them in a circular motion on a clean section of the palette.

Mixing Paint and Extender

Working Paint into Brush Bristles

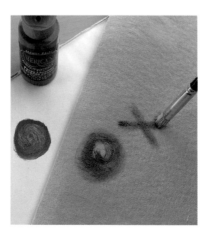

Off-Loading Paint from Brush

One trick to successful stenciling is having only the tiniest amount of paint on your brush bristles. To remove the excess paint, hold the brush upright and with a firm, circular motion, rub the bristles on a folded paper towel. Then, on a clean portion of the paper towel, wipe the brush in an X motion to remove excess paint from the outer bristles.

Applying the Paint

For a smooth stenciled surface, "swirling" is the best technique to use. Hold your stencil brush perpendicular to the project surface and apply the paint by moving the bristle ends in tiny circles. To add texture and depth to a stenciled design, hold the brush perpendicular to the surface, but instead of swirling the bristles, apply the paint by dabbing the brush straight up and down—a process known as "stippling" or "pouncing."

To create shading within each stencil design area, first create sharp, crisp edges by applying paint lightly all the way around the outer edges of the design opening in the stencil. As you work, blend paint into the inner design

Shading with One Color

area but apply less pressure to the brush—and less paint. By varying the pressure you apply to your brush and the amount of time you spend stenciling a given area, you can achieve a wide range of values with a single color.

For added contrast within a design, use more than one color. Let each color dry before applying the next, use a different brush for each color, and leave the stencil in place until you've applied all the colors. (Once you've removed a stencil, it's very difficult to replace it in exactly the same position.)

Shading with Two Colors

To prevent the paint-dampened bristles of your brushes from drying out as you work on a project, keep the brushes in a wet bag until you need to use them again. (See "Wet Bags" on page 9.)

Whiting Out

Before you can stencil on top of a black or dark-colored base coat, you must "white out" the areas where your stenciled designs will appear, or your stenciled colors won't show up on the dark background. Whiting out is easy. Position your stencil, secure it with tape, and create a white background for your stencil colors by stenciling the design with gesso. Leave the stencil in place and allow the gesso to dry. (If you like, you may use a blow dryer to speed up the drying process.) Then stencil your design with the desired colors. Never remove the stencil until you've applied all the colors.

Cleaning and Storing Stencils and Brushes

After using a stencil, you should clean it as soon as possible. The longer the paint remains on the stencil, the harder it will be to remove. Unfortunately, cleaning stencils is hard on them and makes it all too easy to damage them.

One way to clean stencils is with AC's Acrylic Craft Paint Remover. (See "Suppliers" on page 95.) Place the stencil in the sink, pour the cleaner over

it, let the cleaner sit for a minute or two, and then gently scrub off the paint with a scrubber sponge. Rinse the stencil with hot water to remove the cleaner. Another way to clean stencils is to use hot water and a bit of elbow grease. Place the stencil under running hot water and rub it gently with the rough side of a scrubber sponge.

To dry a stencil after cleaning it, place it on a towel and either let it air-dry or pat it dry with a paper towel. Store clean stencils in their original plastic bags, stacking the bags to keep the stencils lying flat.

To clean a stencil brush, first moisten the bristles under running water and scrub them over the surface of a brush scrubber. Next, apply brush cleaner/conditioner to the bristles and scrub them over the brush scrubber again. Then rinse the bristles under water. Repeat until the suds are clear and colorless. Squeeze out the excess water and place the brush on its side to dry.

Color Washes

Color-Washed Surface

A color wash is simply diluted paint and is usually applied on top of an opaque base coat to create a faded, uneven look. To make the wash, first pour a small amount of paint onto your palette. Then, using an artist's brush to transfer water from an artist's water basin to the palette, mix a solution of colored water.

Brush the wash onto the project with an artist's brush. Use long, sweeping strokes that go in the same direction as the strokes in the finish underneath and that extend from one edge of the area you want to wash to the other. If you've never applied a wash before, practice on a sheet of posterboard, using the same colors you plan to use on your project. First apply an opaque base coat to the posterboard and let it dry. Then mix and apply the wash, and let it dry. If the wash color is too light,

just add more paint to the mixture on your palette. To lighten the wash, just add more water.

Sponged Faux Finishes

Sponged Surface

Sponged faux finishes are applied on top of base coats to create variegated textures and colors. To begin, mix paint and faux glazing medium on a palette in the proportions recommended in the project instructions. Use the handle of an artist's brush to mix them together.

Next, put on your gloves. Dampen a natural sea wool sponge with water, wring out the excess moisture, and dip the sponge into the glaze mixture. To work the mixture into the sponge, use a circular motion to rub the sponge on a clean section of your palette. Then dab the sponge onto a paper towel to off-load some of the glaze mixture.

Using a light touch and a stippling motion, sponge the mixture onto the project. Allow the sponged glaze to dry thoroughly. If you like, you may apply more coats, letting each one dry before applying the next.

Antique Finishes

Antique Finish

To create a "distressed" or antique look, first apply one coat of varnish over the opaque base coats on all parts of the project that you'd like to antique. Allow the varnish to dry. Then, working on one small area at a time, use an artist's brush to apply a gel stain over the varnish, brushing in the same direction you did when applying the base coats. While the gel is still wet, use a rag to wipe it. As you wipe, the base-coat colors will darken and acquire an aged look. For a darker finish, apply several coats of the gel stain, wiping each one and allowing it to dry before applying the next.

Crackle Finishes

A crackle finish is one in which thin lines of a base-coat color appear through cracks in a top coat of another color. The crackle finishes in this book were created with crackle size and Venetian plaster.

To create a crackle effect, first apply the layers of acrylic base coat to your project, keeping in mind that the color you use here will be the one that appears through the cracks in the top coat. When the base coat is dry, pour some crackle size onto your palette and use a foam brush to apply the size over the area that you want to crackle. The thinner the coat of crackle size, the smaller the cracks will be and the more subtle the finished effect. For larger, more pronounced cracks, apply a thicker coat. Allow the size to dry to a "firm tack"; this can take anywhere from thirty minutes to four hours.

Next, apply your Venetian plaster over the sized areas of your project. The stronger the contrast between the Venetian plaster color that you use and the color of your base coat, the more noticeable the finished crackle effect will be. The way in which you apply your Venetian plaster will determine the direction of the cracks. For example, long brush strokes, all made in the same direction, will give you long, parallel cracks. Using a piece of wadded-up cheesecloth to stipple into the mixture once you've applied it will break up and vary the directions of the brush strokes and will yield cracks that run in different directions. (See "Applying the Paint" on pages 19–20.)

The only crackled project in this book (see the "All Cracked Up" file cabinet on pages 42–45) also has a negative glazed finish on it. The following section will explain how that finish was applied.

Negative Glazed Finishes

Negative Glazed Crackle Finish

Negative glazed finishes are applied on top of dry crackle finishes to create aged textures and colors. Start by pouring some glazing medium into a mixing tub. Then add a little gel stain, and use the paint-stirring stick to mix it in. Continue adding the gel stain and mixing it in, a little at a time, until you achieve the desired color.

Next, use a chip brush to apply this glaze mixture to your project, working it into the surface well. Then, to create a textured finish and to eliminate brush strokes, wad up a piece of cheesecloth and "pounce" the cheesecloth into the glaze finish. (See "Applying the Paint" on pages 19–20.) Allow the finish to dry thoroughly. If the first application of glaze isn't dark enough to suit you, or if you want to "age" the edges or corners by making them a little darker, you may apply more glaze coats where desired, letting each coat dry before applying the next.

La De Da Dots

La De Da Dots are simply raised dots of paint. To create them, first pour a little paint onto your palette. Then, using one end of an embossing tool, pick up a small amount of paint and apply a dot to the project. To ensure that your dots are raised rather than flat, each time you're ready to make a new dot, pick up more paint from your palette.

Sometimes, beginners have trouble placing dots, bunching them up in some areas and scattering them too far apart in others. *Here's a tip:* Begin by imagining a small diamond or triangle, right in the middle of the area that you want to cover with dots. Apply a dot to each of the diamond's or triangle's corners. Now visualize another diamond or triangle next to the first one. Apply dots to the corners of this second diamond or triangle. By continuing to apply dots to the corners of imaginary diamond or triangle shapes, you'll find that you've scattered your dots evenly.

Make large La De Da Dots by visualizing triangles.

Final Touches

We've always found that it's fun to personalize our projects by signing and dating each piece. When Judy's grandson, Josh, was very young, he would try to say "Judy" and out would come "Jubee" instead, so Judy signs all her work with the word "Ju" and with a stenciled bee—to symbolize the word "Jubee." Jennifer signs each piece with something different. If the piece will be a gift to someone, she often writes a personal message for the recipient. At other times, she just signs "J. Ferguson" and the date.

The next step to completing your project—applying varnish—is very important, as the varnish will protect all the work you've put into your masterpiece. Use a water-based varnish and apply it with a flat artist's brush. To avoid drips and runs, apply at least three thin, even coats, allowing each coat to dry thoroughly before applying the next.

Sign each project.

Painting on Metal

We have been painting on metal for many years. We started with old buckets because our paints adhered to their rough surfaces so well, even after we'd cleaned up the metal. Buckets are still our favorite metal projects; they always look so cute hanging in our booths at crafts shows and conventions.

After several years of experimentation, we finally found water-based primers that adhere well to new metal surfaces as well as to old ones. This discovery opened the door to many new project possibilities: tubs, trash cans, watering cans—almost any metal containers that we could get our hands on.

Before we wrote this book, we had talked about painting filing cabinets for our own personal use, but we were always too busy. Then along came *Painted Whimsies*—and a great opportunity to create and keep the projects we'd always wanted! As we came up with project ideas for this section, we both jumped at the chance to paint the filing cabinet shown on page 42. *Here's a tip:* We've discovered the hard way that every step of preparing metal for painting is very important, so don't cheat by skipping any of them. If you do, you'll just end up having to start over again. If you don't sand the bare metal surface, for example, you may find that when you remove the tape that holds down your stencil, it lifts the base coat right off your project.

"Apple Pickin'" Pail

A simple bucket provides clever storage for magazines, fireplace kindling, or small toys.

Tools and Supplies

See pages 9–14 for more details on tools and supplies.

- 8-quart metal bucket
- 4 wooden ball knobs, 2" diameter
- Scissors
- Miracle Sponge
- Embossing tool
- E6000 adhesive
- Acrylic paints
- Stencils

To reproduce the photographed project, use the DecoArt Americana paints listed below, or substitute them with other acrylic paints for a different look.

- Olive Green (DA56)
- Tomato Red (DA169)
- Taffy Cream (DA05)
- Burnt Umber (DA64)
- Hauser Light Green (DA131)
- Plantation Pine (DA113)
- Marigold (DA194)
- Black (DA67)

If you'd like to reproduce this project exactly as it's shown, use the Stencilled Garden stencils listed here; they're available at specialty stencil stores and through mail-order suppliers. (See "Suppliers" on page 95.) For a different look, just substitute them with other stencils.

Trudy's Apple Pie (TSG194)
Summertime (TSG176)

Instructions

1. Prepare the metal bucket and wooden ball knobs for painting. (See "Preparing Metal" on page 15 and "Preparing Wood" on pages 16–17.)
2. The base coat on the bucket is Olive Green, and the base coat on the wooden ball knobs is Tomato Red. Apply as many coats of paint as necessary to achieve smooth, opaque coverage, but leave the handle and the upper and lower rims of the bucket unpainted. (See "Base-Coat Painting" on page 18.)
3. Stencil the designs. For correct design and color placement, refer to the project photo and to the "Stencil Color Guide" provided above. For detailed stenciling instructions, see "Stenciling" on pages 18–20.

Stencil Color Guide

Trudy's Apple Pie

Taffy Cream, Tomato Red, Burnt Umber,
Hauser Light Green, Plantation Pine

Ladybugs from Summertime

Marigold, Black

4. To create the checks around the upper third of the bucket, first use the scissors to cut a 1" square from the Miracle Sponge. Moisten the cut square with water and wait for it to grow. Then squeeze the excess water from it. Pour a small amount of Tomato Red paint onto your paint palette and dab the moist sponge into the paint. Using the project photo as a placement guide, press the sponge against the bucket to create the checkerboard pattern.
5. Using an embossing tool, apply Tomato Red La De Da Dots around the lower edge of the bucket, and Olive Green La De Da Dots to the wooden ball knobs. (See "La De Da Dots" on pages 22–23.)

6. Sign your bucket and allow all the paint to dry for several days. Then protect your work by applying at least 3 coats of varnish. (See "Final Touches" on page 23.)
7. Using E6000 adhesive, attach the wooden ball knobs to the bottom of the bucket.

Creative Ways to Use a Bucket

Hanging planter
Trash can
Towel holder
Magazine holder
Water bowl for a dog
Kindling container
Container for fireplace ashes
Toy bin
Fruilt or vegetable bin

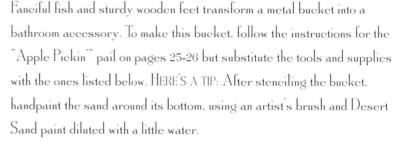

Variation:
"Fishy Bubbles" Bucket

Fanciful fish and sturdy wooden feet transform a metal bucket into a bathroom accessory. To make this bucket, follow the instructions for the "Apple Pickin'" pail on pages 25-26 but substitute the tools and supplies with the ones listed below. HERE'S A TIP: After stenciling the bucket, handpaint the sand around its bottom, using an artist's brush and Desert Sand paint diluted with a little water.

Tools and Supplies

See pages 9–14 for more details on tools and supplies.

- 12-quart metal bucket
- 4 wooden ball knobs, 2" diameter
- Embossing tool
- E6000 adhesive
- Acrylic paints
- Stencil

To reproduce the photographed project, use the DecoArt Americana paints listed below and above right, or substitute them with other acrylic paints for a different look.

- Soft Blue (DA210)
- Yellow Light (DA144)
- Violet Haze (DA197)
- Cadmium Orange (DA14)

- White (DA01)
- Hauser Light Green (DA131)
- Hauser Medium Green (DA132)
- Taffy Cream (DA05)
- Gooseberry Pink (DA27)
- Antique Rose (DA156)
- Wisteria (DA211)
- Cadmium Yellow (DA10)
- Desert Sand (DA77)
- Black (DA67)

If you'd like to reproduce this project exactly as it's shown, use the Stencilled Garden stencil listed here; it's available at specialty stencil stores and through mail-order suppliers. (See "Suppliers" on page 95.) For a different look, just substitute it with another stencil.

- Tropical Fish (TSG802)

"Wild Posies" Trash Can

Cheerful paint and pretty flowers turn a trash can into a clothes hamper.

Tools and Supplies

See pages 9–14 for more details on tools and supplies.

- 10-gallon trash can
- 4 wooden ball knobs, 3" diameter
- Scissors
- Miracle Sponge
- Embossing tool
- E6000 adhesive
- Acrylic paints
- Stencils

To reproduce the photographed project, use the DecoArt Americana paints listed below, or substitute them with other acrylic paints for a different look.

- Moon Yellow (DA07)– 3 bottles
- Country Blue (DA41)
- Hauser Light Green (DA131)
- Evergreen (DA82)
- Santa Red (DA170)
- Black (DA67)

If you'd like to reproduce this project exactly as it's shown, use the Stencilled Garden stencils listed on page 29; they're available at specialty stencil stores and through mail-order suppliers. (See

"Suppliers" on page 95.) For a different look, just substitute them with other stencils.

Wild Posies (TSG190)
Summertime (TSG176)

Instructions

1. Prepare the metal trash can, metal lid, and wooden ball knobs for painting. (See "Preparing Metal" on page 15 and "Preparing Wood" on pages 16–17.)

2. The base coat on the trash can and lid is Moon Yellow, and the base coat on the wooden ball knobs is Country Blue. Apply as many coats of paint as necessary to achieve smooth, opaque coverage, but don't paint the top or bottom rims of the trash can, the rim around the bottom of the lid, or the handles on the trash can and lid. (See "Base-Coat Painting" on page 18.)

3. Stencil the designs. For correct design and color placement, refer to the project photo and to the "Stencil Color Guide" provided above. For detailed stenciling instructions, see "Stenciling" on pages 18–20.

Stencil Color Guide

Flowers from Wild Posies

Country Blue, Hauser Light Green, Evergreen, Moon Yellow

Ladybugs from Summertime

Santa Red, Black

4. To create the checks around the top of the trash can and the edge of the lid, first use the scissors to cut a 1" square from the Miracle Sponge. Moisten the cut square with water and wait for it to grow. Then squeeze the excess water from it. Pour a small amount of Country Blue paint onto your paint palette and dab the moist sponge into the paint. Using the project photo as a placement guide, press the sponge against the trash can and lid to create the checkerboard patterns.

5. Using an embossing tool, apply Black La De Da Dots around the flowers, Moon Yellow La De Da Dots to the flower centers and wooden ball knobs, and Country Blue La De Da Dots along the lower edge of the trash can. (See "La De Da Dots" on pages 22–23.) For correct

placement, refer to the project photo.

6. Sign your trash can and allow all the paint to dry for several days. Then protect your work by applying at least 3 coats of varnish. (See "Final Touches" on page 23.)

7. Using E6000 adhesive, attach the wooden ball knobs to the bottom of the trash can.

Creative Ways to Use a Trash Can

Container for dog or cat food
Container for fireplace ashes
Holder for large garden tools
Clothes hamper
Toy storage

"Toadstool" Tub

Serve beverages with style by stenciling a metal washtub with a charming toadstool landscape.

Tools and Supplies

See pages 9–14 for more details on tools and supplies.

No. 3 metal washtub
4 wooden ball knobs,
    3" diameter
Scissors
Miracle Sponge
Embossing tool

E6000 adhesive
Acrylic paints
Stencils

To reproduce the photographed project, use the DecoArt Americana paints listed below and at right, or substitute them with other acrylic paints for a different look.

Buttermilk (DA03)—2 bottles
Tomato Red (DA169)

Taffy Cream (DA05)
Jade Green (DA57)
Evergreen (DA82)
Driftwood (DA171)
Neutral Grey (DA95)
Antique White (DA58)
Khaki Tan (DA173)
Black (DA67)
Moon Yellow (DA07)
White (DA01)
Deep Periwinkle (DA212)
Country Blue (DA41)

If you'd like to reproduce this project exactly as it's shown, use the Stencilled Garden stencils listed here; they're available at specialty stencil stores and through mail-order suppliers. (See "Suppliers" on page 95.) For a different look, just substitute them with other stencils.

Mushroom Garden (TSG813)
Butterflies (TSG701)

Instructions

1. Prepare the metal washtub and wooden ball knobs for painting. (See "Preparing Metal" on page 15 and "Preparing Wood" on pages 16–17.)
2. The base coat on the washtub is Buttermilk, and the base coat on the wooden ball knobs is Tomato Red. Apply as many coats of paint as necessary to achieve smooth, opaque coverage, but leave the upper and lower rims of the washtub unpainted. (See "Base-Coat Painting" on page 18.)
3. Stencil the designs. For correct design and color placement, refer to the project photo and to the "Stencil Color Guide" provided above. For detailed stenciling instructions, see "Stenciling" on pages 18–20.

Stencil Color Guide

Mushroom Garden

Taffy Cream, Jade Green, Evergreen
Driftwood, Neutral Grey, Tomato Red,
Antique White, Khaki Tan

Butterflies

Black, Moon Yellow, White,
Deep Periwinkle, Country Blue

4. The ground areas under the mushrooms are created with a ¼"-wide stencil brush and Evergreen paint. Before you start to paint each of these areas, off-load your brush, just as you would before stenciling. Then, holding the brush at an angle, apply the paint with a scrubbing motion, going back and forth over each area that you want to paint with this color.
5. To create the checks around the top of the washtub, first use the scissors to cut a 1" square from the Miracle Sponge. Moisten the cut square with water and wait for it to grow. Then squeeze the excess water from it. Pour a small amount of Tomato Red paint onto your paint palette and dab the moist sponge into the paint. Using the project photo as a placement guide, press the sponge against the tub to create the checkerboard pattern.
6. Using an embossing tool, apply White and Black La De Da Dots to the mushrooms and butterflies, and Buttermilk La De Da Dots to the wooden ball knobs. (See "La De Da Dots" on pages 22–23.) For correct placement, refer to the project photo.
7. Sign your washtub and allow all the paint to dry for several days. Then protect your work by applying at least 3 coats of varnish. (See "Final Touches" on page 23.)
8. Using E6000 adhesive, attach the wooden ball knobs to the bottom of the washtub.

"Spring Bouquet" Watering Can

Bright flowers and chunky ball knobs transform a watering can into a kitchen container.

Tools and Supplies

See pages 9–14 for more details on tools and supplies.

   Small metal watering can
   3 wooden ball knobs,
      1½" diameter
   Gesso
   Embossing tool
   E6000 adhesive
   Acrylic paints
   Stencils

To reproduce the photographed project, use the DecoArt Americana paints listed below, or substitute them with other acrylic paints for a different look.

   Black (DA67)
   Santa Red (DA170)
   Hauser Light Green (DA131)
   Evergreen (DA82)
   Marigold (DA194)
   Moon Yellow (DA07)
   Summer Lilac (DA189)
   French Mauve (DA186)
   Pansy Lavender (DA154)
   Raspberry (DA28)

If you'd like to reproduce this project exactly as it's shown, use the Stencilled Garden stencils listed here; they're available at specialty stencil stores and through mail-order suppliers. (See "Suppliers" on page 95.) For a different look, just substitute them with other stencils.

Wild Posies (TSG190)
Kitty Kat Daisies (TSG191)
Girly's Flowers (TSG175)
Ashley's Tea Party (TSG183)

Instructions

1. Prepare the metal watering can and wooden ball knobs for painting. (See "Preparing Metal" on page 15 and "Preparing Wood" on pages 16–17.)
2. The base coat on the watering can is Black, and the base coat on the wooden ball knobs is Santa Red. Apply as many coats of paint as necessary to achieve smooth, opaque coverage, but don't paint the handle or the watering can's upper and lower rims. (See "Base-Coat Painting" on page 18.)
3. Before stenciling on the Black background, use gesso to white out the areas that you plan to stencil. (See "Whiting Out" on page 20.)
4. Stencil the flower designs from each stencil; each stencil requires all of the colors listed for this project except Black. For correct design and color placement, refer to the project photos. For detailed stenciling instructions, see "Stenciling" on pages 18–20.
5. Using an embossing tool, apply Moon Yellow and Santa Red La De Da Dots around the flowers and to their centers, and Black La De Da Dots to the wooden ball knobs. (See "La De Da Dots" on pages 22–23.) For correct placement, refer to the project photos.
6. Sign your watering can and allow all the paint to dry for several days. Then protect your work by applying at least 3 coats of water-resistant exterior varnish. (See "Final Touches" on page 23.)
7. Using E6000 adhesive, attach the wooden ball knobs to the bottom of the watering can.

Creative Ways to Use a Watering Can

Utensil holder
Flower vase
Centerpiece
Potpourri container

Variation:
"Girly's All Checked Out" Watering Can

Tools and Supplies

See pages 9–14 for more details on tools and supplies.

Large watering can
4 wooden ball knobs,
1¾" diameter
Embossing tool
E6000 adhesive
Acrylic paints
Stencils

Showcase your garden cuttings in an eye-catching watering-can vase. To make this watering can, follow the instructions for the "Spring Bouquet" watering can on pages 32-33 but substitute the tools and supplies with the ones listed at right. HERE'S A TIP: To create the checkerboard flowers, first stencil the "Girly's Flowers" design. Leave the stencil in place, set the ¼" checks from the "Little Checks" stencil on top of it, and stencil the checks.

To reproduce the photographed project, use the DecoArt Americana paints listed below, or substitute them with other acrylic paints for a different look.

Wisteria (DA211)—2 bottles
Santa Red (DA170)
Moon Yellow (DA07)
Marigold (DA194)
Hauser Light Green (DA131)
Evergreen (DA82)
Black (DA67)

If you'd like to reproduce this project exactly as it's shown, use the Stencilled Garden stencils listed here; they're available at specialty stencil stores and through mail-order suppliers. (See "Suppliers" on page 95.) For a different look, just substitute them with other stencils.

Girly's Flower Border
(TSG122)
Girly's Flowers (TSG175)
Little Checks (TSG707)
Garden Critters (TSG140)

"Leave a Note" Mailbox

An ordinary mailbox turns whimsical with the addition of playful paints and a decorative post.

Tools and Supplies

See pages 9–14 for more details on tools and supplies.

- A friendly woodworker
- Jigsaw
- 2' length of untreated 1" x 8" lumber
- Metal mailbox
- Wooden post
- 4 wooden ball knobs, 2¼" diameter
- Gesso
- Embossing tool
- E6000 adhesive
- Electric drill
- Drill bit to match screws
- Screwdriver
- Pencil
- Acrylic paints
- Stencils

To reproduce the photographed project, use the DecoArt Americana paints listed below, or substitute them with other acrylic paints for a different look.

Violet Haze (DA197)

Sand (DA04)–2 bottles

Black (DA67)

Moon Yellow (DA07)

Santa Red (DA170)

Hauser Light Green (DA131)

Evergreen (DA82)

Khaki Tan (DA173)

Antique White (DA58)

White (DA01)

Napa Red (DA165)

Charcoal Grey (DA88)

Soft Black (DA155)

Easy Blend Charcoal Grey (DEB28)

If you'd like to reproduce this project exactly as it's shown, use the Stencilled Garden stencils listed here; they're available at specialty stencil stores and through mail-order suppliers. (See "Suppliers" on page 95.) For a different look, just substitute them with other stencils.

Brick Wall (TSG496)

Cherry Pickin' (TSG709S)

Ashley's Tea Party (TSG183)

Cherries Jubilee (TSG184)

Checkerboards (TSG706)

Leave a Note (TSG725)

Instructions

1. Before preparing and painting your metal mailbox, cut a wooden base to fit its underside, using a jigsaw and the 1" x 8" lumber. If you like, you can ask a woodworker to do this for you. (See "Wood—and a Friendly Woodworker" on page 14.)

2. Prepare the metal mailbox, wooden post, wooden ball knobs, and the bottom of the mailbox base for painting. (See "Preparing Metal" on page 15 and "Preparing Wood" on pages 16–17.)

3. Apply as many coats of paint as necessary to achieve smooth, opaque coverage on the mailbox, wooden post, wooden ball knobs, and bottom of the mailbox base. (See "Base-Coat Painting" on page 18.) For correct color placement, refer to the project photos and to the "Base-Coat Color Guide" provided below.

4. Before stenciling on the black mailbox back, use gesso to white out the areas that you plan to stencil. (See "Whiting Out" on page 20.)

5. Stencil all the designs except "Leave a Note." For correct design and color placement, refer to the project photos and to the "Stencil Color Guide" provided on page 37. For detailed stenciling instructions, see "Stenciling" on pages 18–20.

Base-Coat Color Guide

Mailbox Front, Wooden Ball Knobs

Violet Haze

Mailbox Center, Bottom of Wooden Base

Sand

Mailbox Back

Black

Wooden Post (Top to Bottom)

Moon Yellow, Santa Red, Sand, Black, Violet Haze

6. To embellish the stenciled bricks on the center of the mailbox, start by pouring a dime-sized pool of Charcoal Grey onto your paint palette. Add several drops of extender and several drops of water. Using a ¼"-wide, flat artist's brush, apply the Charcoal Grey to the grout areas. Your goal here is to create grout that's unevenly colored. Then, to create the shadow effect around each brick, pour a dime-sized pool of Soft Black onto your palette, and add several drops of extender and several drops of water. Using a long liner brush, paint thin shadows underneath each brick and along one of its sides. (Make sure that the shadows are all on the same sides of the bricks.)

7. Use White paint to stencil the "Leave a Note" design over the bricks. Remove the stencil when the paint has dried and use a paint pen to write a note to your friends and family. Then shield the stenciled design by placing the solid (or "fall-out") portion of the "Leave a Note" stencil over it, and create a shadow around the note by working around the bottom and one side of the shield with Easy Blend Charcoal Grey.

Stencil Color Guide

Project Area	Stencil	Colors
Mailbox Front	Flowers from Ashley's Tea Party	Moon Yellow, Hauser Light Green, Evergreen
Mailbox Center	Brick Wall	Khaki Tan, Antique White
	Leave a Note	White
Mailbox Back	Cherry Pickin'	Santa Red, Napa Red, Hauser Light Green, Evergreen
	Flowers from Ashley's Tea Party	Violet Haze, Hauser Light Green, Evergreen
Wooden Post (Upper Section)	Cherries Jubilee	Santa Red, Napa Red Houser Light Green, Evergreen
Wooden Post (Lower Section)	¾" checks from Checkerboards	Black

8. Using an embossing tool, apply Black La De Da Dots around the flowers, the edge of the mailbox front, and the wooden ball knobs. Apply Santa Red La De Da Dots to the flower centers on the mailbox front, White La De Da Dots to the mailbox back, and Moon Yellow dots to the flower centers on the mailbox back. (See "La De Da Dots" on pages 22–23.) For correct placement, refer to the project photos.

9. Sign your mailbox and allow all the paint to dry for several days. Then protect your work by applying at least 3 coats of exterior varnish. (See "Final Touches" on page 23.)

10. Using E6000 adhesive, attach the wooden ball knobs to the bottom of the wooden base.

11. Center the wooden base on top of the wooden post, with the painted side of the base face down. Using an electric drill and a drill bit that matches the screws, predrill 2 holes through the top of the base and into the top of the post. Insert a screw into each hole, and tighten the screws down with a screwdriver. (You may want to ask a woodworker to do this—and step 12—for you.)

12. Fit the bottom of the mailbox over the wooden base. The mailbox has a row of holes along each of its two long bottom edges. Using the pencil, mark the locations of these holes on the two edges of the wooden base. Remove the mailbox, and use the drill and bit to predrill holes at the marked locations on the base. Place the mailbox on the wooden base again, and attach it to the base by driving screws into the predrilled holes.

Variation:
"Everybirdy Welcome" Mailbox

Keep your garden tools handy with a bright mailbox container for the yard. To prepare and attach the base and post for this mailbox, follow the instructions for the "Leave a Note" mailbox on pages 35-38. HERE'S A TIP: Before stenciling the designs on the Camel-coated mailbox front and on the bottom of the wooden post, apply a sponged faux finish using 1 part Honey Brown paint mixed with 3 parts faux glazing medium. (See "Sponged Faux Finishes" on page 21.)

Tools and Supplies

See pages 9–14 for more details on tools and supplies.

A friendly woodworker

Jigsaw

2' length of untreated 1" x 8" lumber

Metal mailbox

Wooden post

4 wooden ball knobs, 2¼" diameter

Faux glazing medium

Gloves

Natural sea wool sponge

Embossing tool

E6000 adhesive

Electric drill

Drill bit to match screws

Screws

Screwdriver

Pencil

Acrylic paints

Stencils

To reproduce the photo-graphed project, use the DecoArt Americana paints listed below, or substitute them with other acrylic paints for a different look.

> Camel (DA191)
> Limeade (DA206)
> Black (DA67)
> Pansy Lavender (DA154)
> Moon Yellow (DA07)
> Khaki Tan (DA173)
> Burnt Umber (DA64)
> Summer Lilac (DA189)
> Marigold (DA194)
> Country Blue (DA41)
> White (DA01)
> Plantation Pine (DA113)
> Hauser Light Green (DA131)
> Gooseberry Pink (DA27)
> Honey Brown (DA163)

If you'd like to reproduce this project exactly as it's shown, use the Stencilled Garden stencils listed here; they're available at specialty stencil stores and through mail-order suppliers. (See "Suppliers" on page 95.) For a different look, just substitute them with other stencils.

> Wild Animal Print (TSG128)
> Birdhouse Border (TSG520)
> Little Checks (TSG707)
> Sweet Flowerpot (TSG195)
> Curvy Checks (TSG715S)
> Zebra Print (TSG129)
> Checkerboards (TSG706)

Creative Ways to Use a Mailbox

Breadbox
Holder for small garden
    utensils
Drop box for friends
    and family
Office box for incoming
    and outgoing mail
Wedding cardholder

Variation:
"Gone Chicken" Mailbox

A mailbox does kitchen duty, storing bread with farm-themed flair. To make this mailbox, follow the instructions for the "Everybirdy Welcome" mailbox on pages 39-40 but substitute the tools and supplies with the ones listed below. HERE'S A TIP: To create the broken-wire look, stencil the "Chick Chick Wire" design randomly.

Tools and Supplies

See pages 9–14 for more details on tools and supplies.

A friendly woodworker

Metal mailbox

4 wooden ball knobs, 2¼" diameter

Embossing tool

E6000 adhesive

Acrylic paints

Stencils

To reproduce the photographed project, use the DecoArt Americana paints listed below, or substitute them with other acrylic paints for a different look.

Light Buttermilk (DA164)

Moon Yellow (DA07)

Black (DA67)

Tomato Red (DA169)

Cadmium Orange (DA14)

Graphite (DA161)

Hauser Light Green (DA131)

Deep Periwinkle (DA212)

French Vanilla (DA184)

Santa Red (DA170)

Plantation Pine (DA113)

Napa Red (DA165)

White (DA01)

If you'd like to reproduce this project exactly as it's shown, use the Stencilled Garden stencils listed at right; they're available at specialty stencil stores and through mail-order suppliers. (See "Suppliers" on page 95.) For a different look, just substitute them with other stencils.

Penny's Poultry Gone Wild (TSG142)

Cherries Jubilee (TSG184)

Chick Chick Wire (TSG726)

Ashley's Tea Party (TSG183)

Chickie Eggs (TSG727)

"All Cracked Up" File Cabinet

Funky animal prints and wooden ball knobs transform a plain filing cabinet into a snazzy bedside stand.

Tools and Supplies

See pages 9–14 for more details on tools and supplies.

2-drawer metal file cabinet

4 wooden ball knobs, 3" diameter

Transparent graph ruler

Watercolor pencil, any light color

Faux glazing medium

Gloves

Natural sea wool sponge

2 foam brushes

Crackle size

Venetian plaster

Cheesecloth

1-quart mixing tub

Gel stain (DS30)

Stirring stick

2" or 3" chip brush

Embossing tool

E6000 adhesive

4 decorative drawer pulls with screws

Screwdriver

Acrylic paints

Stencils

To reproduce the photographed project, use the DecoArt Americana paints listed below, or substitute them with other acrylic paints for a different look.

Reindeer Moss Green (DA187)

Violet Haze (DA197)

Camel (DA191)

French Vanilla (DA184)

Buttermilk (DA03)

Yellow Ochre (DA08)

Honey Brown (DA163)

Black (DA67)

Raw Sienna (DA93)

Antique Gold (DA09)

Hauser Light Green (DA131)

Plantation Pine (DA113)

If you'd like to reproduce this project exactly as it's shown, use the Stencilled Garden stencils listed here; they're available at specialty stencil stores and through mail-order suppliers. (See "Suppliers" on page 95.) For a different look, just substitute them with other stencils.

Wild Posies (TSG190)

Giraffe Print (TSG230)

Zebra Print (TSG129)

Wild Animal Print (TSG128)

Animal Print (TSG127)

Instructions

1. If your metal file cabinet has handles, remove them. Then prepare the file cabinet and wooden ball knobs for painting. (See "Preparing Metal" on page 15 and "Preparing Wood" on pages 16–17.)

2. The base coat on the entire file cabinet is Reindeer Moss Green, and the base coat on the wooden ball knobs is Violet Haze. Apply as many coats of paint as necessary to achieve smooth, opaque coverage. (See "Base-Coat Painting" on page 18.)

3. Using a transparent graph ruler and a watercolor pencil, measure and mark a 3"-wide border around the top of the cabinet and around each of its 2 side panels. Then measure and mark a 2"-wide border around the front of each drawer.

4. Using the transparent graph ruler and watercolor pencil again, make diagonal lines to mark the 4 triangles at the corners of each side panel. For correct placement of these 8 triangles, refer to the project photo above.

5. Using removable painter's tape, cover the areas just inside all the marked borders on the drawers, top,

and side panels of the cabinet. The tape should leave the borders exposed while protecting the areas that the borders surround. Also protect the 8 marked triangles by placing tape along the outer edges of the diagonal lines. Carefully burnish the edges of each piece of tape.

6. Now you'll apply another base coat to the 2"-wide borders on the cabinet drawers and the 3"-wide borders on each side panel. (You don't need to add another base coat to the borders around the top of the cabinet.) First paint the border around the upper drawer with Camel. Then paint the border around the lower drawer with French Vanilla. Finally, paint the borders around each side panel, starting at the top and working clockwise. On one side panel, the top border is Buttermilk, the right-hand border is Camel, the bottom border is Yellow Ochre, and the left-hand border is French Vanilla. (On the other side panel, as you work clockwise, reverse the colors of the right-hand and left-hand borders.) Apply as many coats of paint as necessary to achieve smooth, opaque coverage over the Reindeer Moss Green base coat. (See

"Base-Coat Painting" on page 18.)

7. On your paint palette, mix 1 part Honey Brown with 3 parts faux glazing medium. Then, while wearing gloves, use a natural sea wool sponge to apply the glaze mixture to all the Camel-painted areas. (See "Sponged Faux Finishes" on page 21.) Allow the glaze mixture to dry. Leave all the tape in place.

8. Stencil the borders first, starting with the four animal-print designs and finishing with the flower designs on the top. For correct design and color placement, refer to the project photos and to the "Stencil Color Guide" provided below. For detailed stenciling

instructions, see "Stenciling" on pages 18–20.

9. When the paint is dry, remove all the tape. You'll stencil the 8 triangles next. Apply new tape to protect the areas outside these triangles, burnish the tape edges well, and stencil the flowers on each triangle. When the paint has dried, remove all the tape.

10. You'll work on the areas inside the borders next, so apply new tape to protect the stenciled borders and triangles and burnish the tape edges well. Then, using a foam brush, apply crackle size to the exposed areas inside the taped borders and triangles only. (See "Crackle Finishes" on page 22.)

Stencil Color Guide

Wild Animal Print
Black

Giraffe Print
Raw Sienna

Zebra Print
Black

Animal Print
Yellow Ochre, Antique Gold, Black

Flowers from Wild Posies
Violet Haze, Hauser Light Green, Plantation Pine

Allow the size to dry to a firm tack.

11. Using another foam brush, apply the Venetian plaster to the sized areas. With a wadded piece of cheese-cloth, stipple the applied plaster. (See "Applying the Paint" on pages 19–20.) Allow it to dry completely. Do not remove the tape yet.

12. Pour some faux glazing medium into the 1-quart mixing tub. Then add a little gel stain. Use a stir-ring stick to mix these ingredients together. Using a 2" or 3" chip brush, apply the glaze mixture over the dry crackled areas. Then elim-inate the brush strokes by using a clean piece of cheesecloth to stipple the wet stain. (See "Negative Glazed Finishes" on page 22.) Allow the glaze to dry completely, then remove all the tape.

13. Using an embossing tool, apply French Vanilla La De Da Dots to the flower centers, Black La De Da Dots randomly around the flowers, and Reindeer Moss Green La De Da Dots to the wooden ball knobs. (See "La De Da Dots" on pages 22–23.) For correct placement, refer to the project photos.

14. Sign your file cabinet and allow all the paint to dry for several days. Then protect your work by applying at least 3 coats of varnish. (See "Final Touches" on page 23.)

15. Using E6000 adhesive, attach the wooden ball knobs to the bottom of the file cabinet.

16. Attach the decorative drawer pulls.

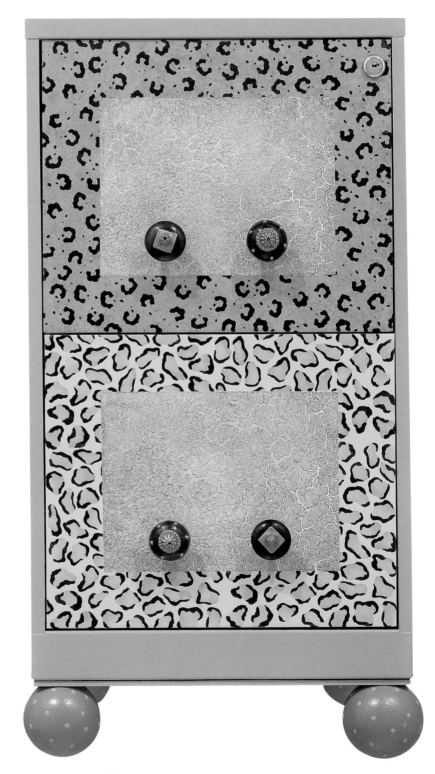

Variation:
"Check and File" Cabinet

File with flair. Subtle checks, freeform flowers, and decorative drawer pulls convert a metal filing cabinet into fun furniture. To make this file cabinet, follow the instructions for the "All Cracked Up" file cabinet on pages 42-45 but substitute the tools and supplies with the ones listed on page 47. HERE'S A TIP: Stencil the "Double Checks" first, and then stencil the other designs over the checkerboard design.

Tools and Supplies

See pages 9–14 for more details on tools and supplies.

2-drawer metal file cabinet
4 wooden ball knobs,
    3" diameter
Embossing tool
E6000 adhesive
4 decorative drawer pulls
    with screws
Screwdriver
Acrylic paints
Stencils

To reproduce the photographed project, use the DecoArt Americana paints listed below, or substitute them with other acrylic paints for a different look.

Sand (DA04)
French Vanilla (DA184)
Moon Yellow (DA07)
Marigold (DA194)
Black (DA67)
Santa Red (DA170)
Country Blue (DA41)
Hauser Light Green (DA131)
Evergreen (DA82)
Khaki Tan (DA173)
Burnt Umber (DA64)
Raw Umber (DA130)
Reindeer Moss Green
    (DA187)
Cadmium Orange (DA14)
French Mauve (DA186)
Burnt Orange (DA16)
Easy Blend Charcoal Grey
    (DEB28)

If you'd like to reproduce this project exactly as it's shown, use the Stencilled Garden

stencils listed here; they're available at specialty stencil stores and through mail-order suppliers. (See "Suppliers" on page 95.) For a different look, just substitute them with other stencils.

Double Checks (TSG713-3)
Garden Critters (TSG140)
Whimsey Critters (TSG828)
Girly's Topiary (TSG244)
Girly's Gone Checked
    (TSG222)
PC Bunny (TSG721)

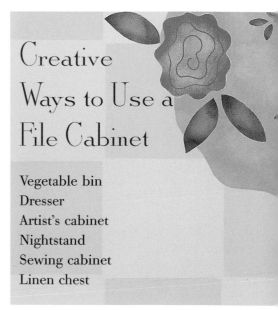

Creative Ways to Use a File Cabinet

Vegetable bin
Dresser
Artist's cabinet
Nightstand
Sewing cabinet
Linen chest

47

Painting on Terra-Cotta

Years ago, Jennifer decided to add a class on painting flowerpots to the classes she teaches at her studio. As usual, she was running behind schedule; she added the class before she started painting a sample to use in it. As the starting date for the class approached, she finally started work on the sample, only to discover that trying to use a flat stencil on a curved and tapered flowerpot wasn't any fun. In fact, ordinary stencils just didn't work; her students were bound to be just as frustrated as she was. She didn't want to give up the class, though, so she went right to the drawing board and solved the problem by creating stencils that were cut to fit curved, tapered pots. These worked so well for the class that she made many more and added them to her stencil line.

Ever since these flowerpot stencils were created, we have had almost too much fun with them. We keep coming up with new ways to use painted terra-cotta pots and saucers: as cookie jars, birdbaths, gumball holders, fishbowls, and more. Who knows what we'll come up with next? We hope that you, too, will have fun with these projects and let your own imaginations soar.

"Sweet Strawberry Divine" Flowerpot

Charming ball-knob feet add height and visual punch to a terra-cotta flowerpot.

Tools and Supplies

See pages 9–14 for more details on tools and supplies.

8½" terra-cotta flowerpot

8" terra-cotta saucer

4 wooden ball knobs, 1½" diameter

Embossing tool

E6000 adhesive

Acrylic paints

Stencils

To reproduce the photographed project, use the DecoArt Americana paints listed below, or substitute them with other acrylic paints for a different look.

French Vanilla (DA184)

Tomato Red (DA169)

Napa Red (DA165)

Plantation Pine (DA113)

Hauser Light Green (DA131)

Moon Yellow (DA07)

Marigold (DA194)

Black (DA67)

If you'd like to reproduce this project exactly as it's shown, use the Stencilled Garden stencils listed here; they're available at specialty stencil stores and through mail-order suppliers. (See "Suppliers" on page 95.) For a different look, just substitute them with other stencils.

Strawberry Pot (TSG197)

Wild Posies (TSG190)

Summertime (TSG176)

Instructions

1. Prepare the terra-cotta flowerpot, terra-cotta saucer, and wooden ball knobs for painting. (See "Preparing Terra-Cotta" on pages 15–16 and "Preparing Wood" on pages 16–17.)

2. Apply as many coats of paint as necessary to achieve smooth, opaque coverage. (See "Base-Coat Painting" on page 18.) For correct color placement, refer to the project photo and to the "Base-Coat Color Guide" provided at right. *Here's a tip:* When applying the base coat to the flowerpot, first paint the outside, beneath the rim, and allow the paint to dry completely. Then paint the inside and outside of the rim. Leave the inside of the pot, beneath the rim, unpainted.

3. Stencil the designs. For correct design and color placement, refer to the project photo and to the "Stencil Color Guide" provided at right. For detailed stenciling instructions, see "Stenciling" on pages 18–20.

4. Using an embossing tool, apply Black La De Da Dots randomly around the flowers, Tomato Red La De Da Dots to the flower centers and wooden ball knobs, and French Vanilla La De Da Dots around the exterior rim of the saucer. (See "La De Da Dots" on pages 22–23.) For correct placement, refer to the project photo.

5. Sign your flowerpot and allow all the paint to dry for several days. Then protect your work by applying at least 3 coats of water-resistant exterior varnish. (See "Final Touches" on page 23.) *Here's a tip:* Coating the entire flowerpot and saucer with varnish, including the unpainted surfaces, will help prevent the paint from bubbling.

6. Using E6000 adhesive, attach the wooden ball knobs to the bottom of the saucer.

Base-Coat Color Guide

Flowerpot (Outside, Beneath Rim)

French Vanilla

Flowerpot Rim

Tomato Red

Saucer

Tomato Red

Wooden Ball Knobs

French Vanilla

Stencil Color Guide

Strawberry Pot

Tomato Red, Napa Red, Hauser Light Green, Plantation Pine

Flowers from Wild Posies

Moon Yellow, Marigold, Hauser Light Green, Plantation Pine

Ladybugs from Summertime

Marigold, Black

Variation:
"Color Me Bright" Flowerpot

Serve bread, candies, or other treats with a flourish in painted terra-cotta. To make this flowerpot, follow the instructions for the "Sweet Strawberry Divine" flowerpot on pages 49–50 but substitute the tools and supplies with the ones listed at right.

Tools and Supplies

See pages 9–14 for more details on tools and supplies.

    8½" terra-cotta flowerpot
    8" terra-cotta saucer
    4 wooden ball knobs,
       1½" diameter
    Scissors
    Miracle Sponge
    Embossing tool
    E6000 adhesive
    Acrylic paints
    Stencil

To reproduce the photographed project, use the DecoArt Americana paints listed below, or substitute them with other acrylic paints for a different look.

    Olive Green (DA56)
    Summer Lilac (DA186)
    Black (DA67)
    Marigold (DA194)
    Moon Yellow (DA07)
    Pansy Lavender (DA154)
    Hauser Light Green (DA131)
    Evergreen (DA82)

If you'd like to reproduce this project exactly as it's shown, use the Stencilled Garden stencil listed here; it's available at specialty stencil stores and through mail-order suppliers. (See "Suppliers" on page 95.) For a different look, just substitute it with another stencil.

    Ashley's Tea Party (TSG183)

"Hippity Hop" Cookie Jar

An upturned saucer with whimsical finial handle becomes the lid for this terra-cotta cookie jar.

Tools and Supplies

See pages 9–14 for more details on tools and supplies.

8½" terra-cotta flowerpot
9" terra-cotta saucer
4 wooden ball knobs,
   1½" diameter
Wooden finial, 4¼" long
Embossing tool
E6000 adhesive
Acrylic paints
Stencils

To reproduce the photographed project, use the DecoArt Americana paints listed below, or substitute them with other acrylic paints for a different look.

Reindeer Moss Green
   (DA187)—2 bottles
Deep Periwinkle (DA212)—
   2 bottles
Country Blue (DA41)
Jade Green (DA57)
Plantation Pine (DA113)
White (DA01)
Dusty Rose (DA25)
Black (DA67)
Cadmium Orange (DA14)
Burnt Orange (DA16)
Moon Yellow (DA07)

If you'd like to reproduce this project exactly as it's shown, use the Stencilled Garden stencils listed here; they're available at specialty stencil stores and through mail-order suppliers. (See "Suppliers" on page 95.) For a different look, just substitute them with other stencils.

Wild Posies (TSG190)
Springtime (TSG182)

Instructions

1. Prepare the terra-cotta flowerpot, terra-cotta saucer, wooden ball knobs, and wooden finial for painting. (See "Preparing Terra-Cotta" on pages 15–16 and "Preparing Wood" on pages 16–17.)

2. Apply as many coats of paint as necessary to achieve smooth, opaque coverage on all project parts. (See "Base-Coat Painting" on page 18.) For correct color placement, refer to the project photo and to the "Base-Coat Color Guide" provided at right. *Here's a tip:* When applying the base coat to the flowerpot, first paint the outside, beneath the rim, and allow the paint to dry thoroughly. Then paint the rim and the inside of the flowerpot.

3. Stencil the designs. For correct design and color placement, refer to the project photo and to the "Stencil Color Guide" provided at right. For detailed stenciling instructions, see "Stenciling" on pages 18–20.

4. Using an embossing tool, apply Black La De Da Dots randomly around the flowers, and Deep Periwinkle La De Da Dots to the flower centers on the flowerpot rim and saucer. Apply Moon Yellow La De Da Dots to the flower centers on the outside of the flowerpot, and Reindeer Moss Green La De Da Dots to the wooden ball knobs. Apply White La De Da Dots to the Reindeer Moss Green areas on the finial. (See "La De Da Dots" on pages 22–23.) For correct placement, refer to the project photo.

5. Sign your cookie jar and allow all the paint to dry for several days. Then protect your work by applying at least 3 coats of varnish to all the surfaces.

(See "Final Touches" on page 23.)

6. Using E6000 adhesive, attach the wooden ball knobs to the bottom of the flowerpot and attach the finial to the bottom of the saucer. *Here's a tip:* Whenever you use a painted flowerpot to store food, place the food in a plastic bag before placing it in the container, or the food may "leak" through the hole in the bottom. To serve food such as dinner rolls in a flowerpot, cover the inside of the pot with paper napkins.

Base-Coat Color Guide

Flowerpot (Outside, Beneath Rim)
Reindeer Moss Green

Flowerpot (Inside and Rim)
Deep Periwinkle

Saucer and Wooden Ball Knobs
Deep Periwinkle

Finial (Top to Bottom)
Reindeer Moss Green, Deep Periwinkle, Reindeer Moss Green, Deep Periwinkle, Reindeer Moss Green

Stencil Color Guide

Flowers from Wild Posies
Country Blue, Deep Periwinkle, Jade Green, Plantation Pine

Bunnies and Carrots from Springtime
White, Dusty Rose, Black, Cadmium Orange, Burnt Orange, Jade Green, Plantation Pine

Variation:
"La De Da" Canister Trio

Flowerpots convert to food canisters with the addition of British-knob handles. To make these canisters, follow the instructions for the "Hippity Hop" cookie jar on pages 52-53 but substitute the tools and supplies with the ones listed below.

To reproduce the photographed project, use the DecoArt Americana paints listed below, or substitute them with other acrylic paints for a different look.

> French Mauve (DA186)
> Moon Yellow (DA07)
> Jade Green (DA57)
> Black (DA67)
> Violet Haze (DA197)
> Payne's Grey (DA167)
> Evergreen (DA82)
> Hauser Light Green (DA131)
> Antique Mauve (DA162)
> Marigold (DA194)
> Santa Red (DA170)
> Napa Red (DA165)

If you'd like to reproduce this project exactly as it's shown, use the Stencilled Garden stencils listed here; they're available at specialty stencil stores and through mail-order suppliers. (See "Suppliers" on page 95.) For a different look, just substitute them with other stencils.

> Girly's Flowers (TSG175)
> Cherries Jubilee (TSG184)
> Ashley's Tea Party (DA183)
> Wild Posies (TSG190)
> Kitty Kat Daisies (TSG191)

Tools and Supplies

See pages 9–14 for more details on tools and supplies.

3" terra-cotta flowerpot	3 British knobs,
4" terra-cotta flowerpot	1⅝" diameter
6" terra-cotta flowerpot	Embossing tool
3" terra-cotta saucer	E6000 adhesive
4" terra-cotta saucer	Acrylic paints
6" terra-cotta saucer	Stencils

"Buggy Bugs" Bird Feeder

A terra-cotta flowerpot and oversized saucer tempt feathered visitors with stenciled bugs.

Tools and Supplies

See pages 9–14 for more details on tools and supplies.

- 6" terra-cotta flowerpot
- 10" terra-cotta saucer
- Large, empty bottle with lid
- Faux glazing medium
- Gloves
- Natural sea wool sponge
- E6000 adhesive
- Acrylic paints
- Stencils

To reproduce the photographed project, use the DecoArt Americana paints listed below, or substitute them with other acrylic paints for a different look.

- Country Blue (DA41)
- White (DA01)—2 bottles
- Hauser Light Green (DA131)
- Evergreen (DA82)
- Ice Blue—Metallic (DA75)
- Green Pearl—Metallic (DA122)
- Moon Yellow (DA07)
- Marigold (DA194)
- Black (DA67)
- Charcoal Grey (DA88)
- Santa Red (DA170)
- Summer Lilac (DA189)
- Pansy Lavender (DA154)

If you'd like to reproduce this project exactly as it's shown, use the Stencilled Garden stencils listed here; they're available at specialty stencil stores and through mail-order suppliers. (See "Suppliers" on page 95.) For a different look, just substitute them with other stencils.

Buggy Border (TSG827)

Garden Critters (TSG140)

Stencil Color Guide

Buggy Border

Ice Blue—Metallic, Green Pearl—Metallic, Moon Yellow, Marigold, Black, Charcoal Grey, Santa Red, Summer Lilac, Pansy Lavender, Hauser Light Green, Evergreen

Ladybug from Garden Critters

Black, Santa Red

Instructions

1. Prepare the terra-cotta flowerpot and saucer for painting. (See "Preparing Terra-Cotta" on pages 15–16.)

2. The base coat on the flowerpot and saucer is a mixture of Country Blue and White. Start by filling four-fifths of the large, empty bottle with White paint. Then add Country Blue to create a very pale blue color, shaking the mixture well. (When dry, acrylic colors are darker than they appear in their bottles. To test a color, brush some of the paint onto a piece of paper and let it dry.)

3. Apply as many coats of the pale blue paint as necessary to achieve smooth, opaque coverage on the entire saucer, the outside of the flowerpot, and the inside and outside of the flowerpot rim. (See "Base-Coat Painting" on page 18.)

4. On your paint palette, mix 1 part White paint with 1 part faux glazing medium. Put on the gloves. Then, using a natural sea wool sponge, lightly sponge the glaze mixture onto the flowerpot and saucer. (See "Sponged Faux Finishes" on page 21.)

5. Some of the grass blades on the flowerpot rim are Hauser Light Green; others are Evergreen. To paint them, start by pouring a nickel-sized pool of Hauser Light Green paint onto your paint palette. Add a couple drops of extender to the paint and enough water to make it the texture of light cream. Diluting the paint in this manner will help you achieve smooth, continuous brush strokes. Then turn the flowerpot upside down. To paint each Hauser Light Green blade, hold the long liner brush perpendicular to the flowerpot's surface. Start at the edge of the rim that touches your work surface and brush upward, lifting the brush up at the end of the stroke. When the paint is dry, repeat this step to add Evergreen blades.

6. Stencil the designs. For correct design and color placement, refer to the project photos and to the "Stencil Color Guide" provided above. For detailed stenciling instructions, see "Stenciling" on pages 18–20.

7. Sign your bird feeder and allow all the paint to dry for several days. Then, to protect your work when it's outdoors, apply at least 3 coats of exterior varnish to all its surfaces, both inside and out. (See "Final Touches" on page 23.) *Here's a tip:* Coating the inside and outside of the flowerpot with varnish will help prevent the paint from bubbling.

8. Using E6000 adhesive, attach the saucer to the bottom of the flowerpot.

"Blowing Bubbles" Gumball Holder

Pair a flowerpot with a fishbowl to make this delightful candy container.

Tools and Supplies

See pages 9–14 for more details on tools and supplies.

- 6" terra-cotta flowerpot
- 4" terra-cotta saucer
- Wooden ball knob, 1¾" diameter
- No. 6 glass fishbowl
- Embossing tool
- E6000 adhesive
- Acrylic paints
- Stencils

To reproduce the photographed project, use the DecoArt Americana paints listed below, or substitute them with other acrylic paints for a different look.

- Buttermilk (DA03)
- Moon Yellow (DA07)
- Berry Red (DA19)
- Hauser Light Green (DA131)
- Hauser Medium Green (DA132)
- Black (DA67)
- Country Blue (DA41)
- Evergreen (DA82)

If you'd like to reproduce this project exactly as it's shown, use the Stencilled Garden stencils listed here; they're available at specialty stencil stores and through mail-order suppliers. (See "Suppliers" on page 95.) For a different look, just substitute them with other stencils.

Summertime (TSG176)

Ashley's Tea Party (TSG183)

Instructions

1. Prepare the terra-cotta flowerpot, terra-cotta saucer, and wooden ball knob for painting. (See "Preparing Terra-Cotta" on pages 15–16 and "Preparing Wood" on pages 16–17.)

2. Apply as many coats of paint as necessary to achieve smooth, opaque coverage on the entire saucer, the inside of the flowerpot, and the inside and outside of the flowerpot rim. (See "Base-Coat Painting" on page 18.) For correct color placement, refer to the project photo and to the "Base-Coat Color Guide" provided at right. *Here's a tip:* When applying the base coat to the flowerpot, first paint the outside, beneath the rim, and allow the paint to dry thoroughly. Then paint the inside and outside of the rim. Leave the inside of the pot, beneath the rim, unpainted.

3. Stencil the designs. For correct design and color placement, refer to the project photo and to the "Stencil Color Guide" provided below. For detailed stenciling instructions, see "Stenciling" on pages 18–20.

4. Using an embossing tool, apply Black La De Da Dots randomly around the flowers, Moon Yellow La De Da Dots to the flower centers and to the wooden ball knob, and Berry Red La De Da Dots to the rim of the saucer. (See "La De Da Dots" on pages 22–23.) For correct placement, refer to the project photo.

5. Sign your gumball holder and allow all the paint to dry for several days. Then protect your work by applying at least 3 coats of varnish to the entire project, including the inside of the flowerpot. (See "Final Touches" on page 23.)

6. Using E6000 adhesive, attach the No. 6 glass fishbowl to the bottom of the flowerpot and attach the wooden ball knob to the inside of the saucer.

Base-Coat Color Guide

Flowerpot (Outside, Beneath Rim)

Buttermilk

Flowerpot Rim and Saucer

Moon Yellow

Wooden Ball Knob

Berry Red

Stencil Color Guide

Watermelon and Ladybugs from Summertime

Berry Red, Hauser Light Green, Hauser Medium Green, Black

Flowers from Ashley's Tea Party

Country Blue, Hauser Light Green, Evergreen

Variation:
"Home Run Derby" Fishbowl

A flowerpot base gives this clever fishbowl a striking silhouette. To make the terra-cotta base for this fishbowl, follow the instructions for the "Blowing Bubbles" gumball holder on pages 57-58 but substitute the tools and supplies with the ones listed at right.

Tools and Supplies

See pages 9–14 for more details on tools and supplies.

6" terra-cotta flowerpot
No. 10 glass fishbowl
Embossing tool
E6000 adhesive
Acrylic paints
Stencils

To reproduce the photographed project, use the DecoArt Americana paints listed below, or substitute them with other acrylic paints for a different look.

Desert Sand (DA77)
Berry Red (DA19)
White (DA01)
Burnt Umber (DA64)
Black (DA67)

If you'd like to reproduce this project exactly as it's shown, use the Stencilled Garden stencils listed here; they're available at specialty stencil stores and through mail-order suppliers. (See "Suppliers" on page 95.) For a different look, just substitute them with other stencils.

Play Ball (TSG185)
Garden Critters (TSG140)

"Bottoms Up" Birdbath

Flowerpots turned upside down add layers of fun to this birdbath charmer.

Tools and Supplies

See pages 9–14 for more details on tools and supplies.

- 12" terra-cotta flowerpot
- 14½" terra-cotta flowerpot
- 17" terra-cotta flowerpot
- 18" terra-cotta saucer
- E6000 adhesive
- Acrylic paints
- Stencils

To reproduce the photographed project, use the DecoArt Americana paints listed below and on page 61, or substitute them with other acrylic paints for a different look.

- Olive Green (DA56)—2 to 3 bottles
- Buttermilk (DA03)—3 to 4 bottles
- Gooseberry Pink (DA27)
- White (DA01)
- Taffy Cream (DA05)
- Moon Yellow (DA07)
- Marigold (DA194)
- Burnt Orange (DA16)
- Oxblood (DA139)
- Winter Blue (DA190)
- Williamsburg Blue (DA40)
- Santa Red (DA170)
- Black (DA67)
- Charcoal Grey (DA88)
- Antique Maroon (DA160)

Soft Black (DA155)
Violet Haze (DA197)
Hauser Light Green (DA131)
Evergreen (DA82)
Honey Brown (DA163)
Camel (DA191)

If you'd like to reproduce this project exactly as it's shown, use the Stencilled Garden stencils listed here; they're available at specialty stencil stores and through mail-order suppliers. (See "Suppliers" on page 95.) For a different look, just substitute them with other stencils.

Bottom's Up (TSG723)
Bumble Bee (TSG729)
Mama Lady Bug (TSG724)
Giraffe Print (TSG230)
Folk Art Tulips (TSG240)
Zebra Print (TSG129)
Buzzy Bee Border (TSG825)
Jubee's Cow Spots (TSG231)

Instructions

1. Prepare the terra-cotta flowerpots and saucer for painting. (See "Preparing Terra-Cotta" on pages 15–16.)

2. Apply as many coats of paint as necessary to achieve smooth, opaque coverage on the entire saucer, the outside of each flowerpot, and the inside and outside of each flowerpot rim. (See "Base-Coat Painting" on page

18.) For correct color placement, refer to the project photo and to the "Base-Coat Color Guide" provided below. *Here's a tip:* When applying the base coats to each flowerpot, first paint the outside, beneath the rim, and allow the paint to dry thoroughly. Then paint the inside and the outside of the rim. Leave the inside of the pot, beneath the rim, unpainted.

3. Stencil the designs. For correct design and color placement, refer to the project photo and to the "Stencil Color Guide" provided on page 62. (The stencils are listed as they appear on the birdbath, from the inside of the saucer on top to the largest flowerpot on the bottom.) For detailed stenciling instructions, see "Stenciling" on pages 18–20.

Base-Coat Color Guide

18" Saucer
Olive Green

12" Flowerpot (Outside, Beneath Rim)
Buttermilk

12" Flowerpot Rim
Gooseberry Pink

14½" Flowerpot (Outside, Beneath Rim)
Buttermilk

14½" Flowerpot Rim
Olive Green

17" Flowerpot (Outside, Beneath Rim)
Buttermilk

17" Flowerpot Rim
White

4. Sign your birdbath and allow all the paint to dry for several days. Then, to protect your work when it's outdoors, apply at least 3 coats of water-resistant exterior varnish to all its surfaces, including the inside of each flowerpot. (See "Final Touches" on page 23.) *Here's a tip:* Coating all the terra-cotta surfaces with varnish,

both inside and out, will help prevent the paint from bubbling.

5. Using E6000 adhesive, attach the saucer to the bottom of the 12" flowerpot as shown in the project photo. To assemble your birdbath, simply stack the flowerpots; you don't need to glue them together.

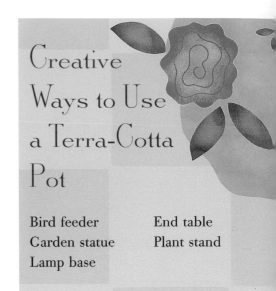

Creative Ways to Use a Terra-Cotta Pot

Bird feeder   End table
Carden statue   Plant stand
Lamp base

Stencil Color Guide

Project Area	Stencil	Colors
Saucer	Bottom's Up	Taffy Cream, Moon Yellow, Marigold, Burnt Orange, Oxblood, Winter Blue, Williamsburg Blue
12" Flowerpot (Exterior, Beneath Rim)	Mama Lady Bug	Santa Red, Black
	Bumble Bee	Moon Yellow, Marigold, Black, Charcoal Grey
12" Flowerpot Rim	Giraffe Print	Antique Maroon, Soft Black
14½" Flowerpot (Exterior, Beneath Rim)	Folk Art Tulips	Violet Haze, Hauser Light Green, Evergreen
14½" Flowerpot Rim	Zebra Print	Black
17" Flowerpot (Exterior, Beneath Rim)	Buzzy Bee Border	Honey Brown, Camel, Black, Moon Yellow, Marigold, Charcoal Grey, Evergreen
17" Flowerpot Rim	Jubee's Cow Spots	Black

"Garden Mouse" Stepping-Stone

Accent your garden path, create a decorative doorstop, or support an outdoor flowerpot with a stenciled stepping-stone.

Tools and Supplies

See pages 9–14 for more details on tools and supplies.

- 16" octagonal brick stepping-stone
- Embossing tool
- Acrylic paints
- Stencils

To reproduce the photographed project, use the DecoArt Americana paints listed below and top right, or substitute them with other acrylic paints for a different look.

- Eggshell (DA153)—2 bottles
- Taffy Cream (DA05)
- Jade Green (DA57)
- Plantation Pine (DA113)
- Buttermilk (DA03)
- Plum (DA175)
- Black Plum (DA172)
- Hauser Light Green (DA131)
- Evergreen (DA82)
- Neutral Grey (DA95)
- Charcoal Grey (DA88)
- Black (DA67)
- Easy Blend Charcoal Grey (DEB28)

If you'd like to reproduce this project exactly as it's shown, use the Stencilled Garden stencils listed here; they're available at specialty stencil stores and through mail-order suppliers. (See "Suppliers" on page 95.) For a different look, just substitute them with other stencils.

- English Ivy (TSG917)
- Garden Gloves (TSG213)
- Mouser (TSG722)
- Wild Posies (TSG190)
- Checkerboards (TSG706)

Instructions

1. Prepare the brick stepping-stone for painting. (See "Preparing Terra-Cotta" on pages 15–16.)
2. Apply as many Eggshell base coats as necessary to achieve smooth, opaque

coverage on the entire stepping-stone. (See "Base-Coat Painting" on page 18.)

3. Stencil the designs. For correct design and color placement, refer to the project photo and to the "Stencil Color Guide" provided at right. For detailed stenciling instructions, see "Stenciling" on pages 18–20.

4. To create the shadow effects around the gloves, mouse, and ivy, use a ¼"-wide stencil brush and Easy Blend Charcoal Grey to paint the shadows freehand after the stencils are removed. Hold the brush at an angle and scrub along one edge of each painted design. (Make sure you place the shadows on the same side of each design.)

5. Using an embossing tool, apply Buttermilk La De Da Dots to the flower centers on the gloves. (See "La De Da Dots" on pages 22–23.)

6. Sign your stepping-stone and allow all the paint to dry for several days. Then protect your work by applying at least 3 coats of exterior varnish to the entire stepping-stone. (See "Final Touches" on page 23.)

Stencil Color Guide

English Ivy
Taffy Cream, Jade Green, Plantation Pine

Garden Gloves
Buttermilk, Plum, Black Plum, Hauser Light Green, Evergreen

Mouser
Neutral Grey, Charcoal Grey, Black

Wild Posies
Plum, Black Plum, Hauser Light Green, Evergreen

¾" Checks from Checkerboards
Plum

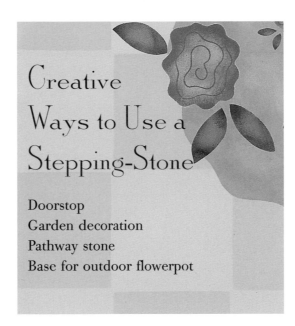

Creative Ways to Use a Stepping-Stone

Doorstop
Garden decoration
Pathway stone
Base for outdoor flowerpot

Variation:

"Boatin' in the U.S.A." Stepping-Stone

Summertime stepping-stone: Celebrate the warm weather with a stenciled watermelon and jaunty flag. To make this stepping stone, follow the instructions for the "Garden Mouse" stepping-stone on pages 63-64 but substitute the tools and supplies with the ones listed at right.

Tools and Supplies

See pages 9–14 for more details on tools and supplies.

- 12" round stepping-stone
- Embossing tool
- Acrylic paints
- Stencils

To reproduce the photographed project, use the DecoArt Americana paints listed below, or substitute them with other acrylic paints for a different look.

- Winter Blue (DA190)
- Santa Red (DA170)
- Napa Red (DA165)
- Marigold (DA194)
- Moon Yellow (DA07)
- Hauser Light Green (DA131)
- Hauser Medium Green (DA132)
- Admiral Blue (DA213)
- White (DA01)
- Black (DA67)

If you'd like to reproduce this project exactly as it's shown, use the Stencilled Garden stencils listed here; they're available at specialty stencil stores and through mail-order suppliers. (See "Suppliers" on page 95.) For a different look, just substitute them with other stencils.

- American Pie (TSG238)
- Girly's Flowers (TSG175)
- Garden Critters (TSG140)
- Checkerboards (TSG706)

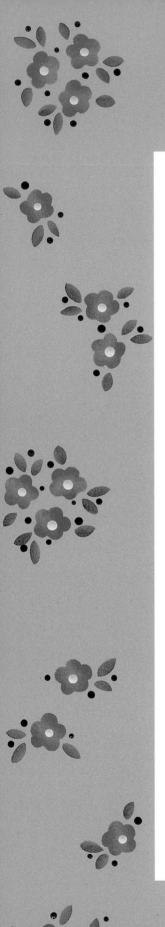

Painting on Wood

We first started painting on wood, and wooden projects continue to be our passion. (If you're new to stenciling, this material is a great choice; it's easy to paint and very forgiving.) When we can't find ready-made wooden items to paint, we pass our concepts and patterns to our wonderful local woodworker, Jay, who somehow transforms them into what we want. Of course, we don't always get around to painting these projects right away, but they're there in case we ever have time.

As we worked on *Painted Whimsies,* we went through all the wooden projects that Jay has made for us over the years and chose ones to paint. We pushed ourselves—as we always do—to use new colors. It's all too easy to get "stuck" on certain colors, and we wanted to create great color combinations for you.

Several years ago we discovered wooden ball knobs, which come in various sizes and which we thought would look cute attached to painted flowerpots and cookie jars. But we couldn't just leave it at that; we started attaching them to everything. We refer to them as "feet"—and we think everything should have feet!

As we investigated sources for ball knobs, we found other wooden objects that we could use as feet or knobs. That's how we got started with finials, beehives, and British knobs. We're still searching for more items of this kind. Who knows what we'll find next?

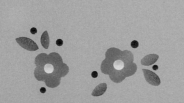

"French Country" Serving Tray

A plain wooden tray turns stylish with the addition of simple handles, feet, and a classic motif.

Tools and Supplies

See pages 9–14 for more details on tools and supplies.

Wooden serving tray
4 wooden ball knobs, 1¾" diameter
Embossing tool

E6000 adhesive
2 metal handles with screws
Screwdriver
Acrylic paints
Stencils

To reproduce the photographed project, use the DecoArt Americana paints listed at right and on page 68, or substitute them with other acrylic paints for a different look.

Light Buttermilk (DA164)—
2 bottles
French Vanilla (DA184)
Country Blue (DA41)
Yellow Ochre (DA08)
Antique Gold (DA09)
Payne's Grey (DA167)

Country Red (DA18)
Deep Burgundy (DA128)
Khaki Tan (DA173)
Charcoal Grey (DA88)
Soft Black (DA155)

If you'd like to reproduce this project exactly as it's shown, use the Stencilled Garden stencils listed here; they're available at specialty stencil stores and through mail-order suppliers. (See "Suppliers" on page 95.) For a different look, just substitute them with other stencils.

Frenchy (TSG143)
Patricia Ann's Petals (TSG226)

Instructions

1. Prepare the wooden serving tray and wooden ball knobs for painting. (See "Preparing Wood" on pages 16–17.)

2. Apply as many coats of paint as necessary to achieve smooth, opaque coverage on the serving tray and wooden ball knobs. (See "Base-Coat Painting" on page 18.) For correct color placement, refer to the project photos and to the "Base-Coat Color Guide" provided on page 69.

3. To create the stripes on the inside and outside of each edging strip, start by pouring a small amount of Yellow Ochre onto your paint palette. Dilute the paint with water. Then use a ¾"-wide artist's brush to paint the stripes freehand, spacing them approximately 1" apart. (These stripes should be soft and whimsical in appearance rather than precise.) For best results, use a newer brush with bristles that haven't been flared.

4. Stencil the designs. For correct design and color placement, refer to the project photos and to the "Stencil Color Guide" provided at right. For detailed stenciling instructions, see "Stenciling" on pages 18–20.

5. Using an embossing tool, apply Yellow Ochre La De Da Dots to the inside bottom of the tray, and French Vanilla La De Da Dots to the tops of the edging panels and to the wooden ball knobs. (See "La De Da Dots" on pages 22–23.)

6. Sign your tray and allow all the paint to dry for several days. Then protect your work by applying at least 3 coats of varnish. (See "Final Touches" on page 23.)

7. Using E6000 adhesive, attach the wooden ball knobs to the bottom of the tray.

8. Attach the metal handles to the tops of the two short edging strips.

Base-Coat Color Guide

Inside of Bottom
Light Buttermilk

Edging Strips, Outside of Bottom
French Vanilla

Tops of Edging Strips
Country Blue

Stencil Color Guide

Frenchy
French Vanilla, Yellow Ochre, Antique Gold, Payne's Grey, Country Blue, Country Red, Deep Burgundy, Khaki Tan, Charcoal Grey, Soft Black

Patricia Ann's Petals
Country Blue, Payne's Grey

Variation:
"Breakfast in Bed" Tray

Make breakfast in bed even more enticing by serving it on a tea-themed tray, which can do additional duty as a writing desk or book rest. To make this tray, follow the instructions for the "French Country" serving tray on pages 67–69 but substitute the tools and supplies with the ones listed at right.

Tools and Supplies

See pages 9–14 for more details on tools and supplies.

Wooden breakfast tray
Embossing tool
2 clear-glass decorative drawer pulls with screws
Electric drill
Drill bit to match screws
Acrylic paints
Stencils

To reproduce the photographed project, use the DecoArt Americana paints listed at top right, or substitute them with other acrylic paints for a different look.

Soft Sage (DA207)
Summer Lilac (DA189)
Pansy Lavender (DA154)
Royal Purple (DA150)
Black (DA67)
Jade Green (DA57)
Evergreen (DA82)
Dark Chocolate (DA65)
Asphaltum (DA180)
Marigold (DA194)
Easy Blend Charcoal
    Grey (DEB28)
Moon Yellow (DA07)
Arbor Green (DA209)

If you'd like to reproduce this project exactly as it's shown, use the Stencilled Garden stencils listed here; they're available at specialty stencil stores and through mail-order suppliers. (See "Suppliers" on page 95.) For a different look, just substitute them with other stencils.

Whimsey Topiaries (TSG243)
Two for Tea (TSG237)
Folk Art Tulips (TSG240)
Checkerboards (TSG706)
Ashley's Tea Party (TSG183)

"Monarch Village" Butterfly House

Invite butterflies to linger by giving them a colorful home in your garden.

Tools and Supplies

See pages 9–14 for more details on tools and supplies.

Wooden butterfly house
Wooden post
A friendly woodworker
2" or 3" chip brush
Gel stain (DS30)
Acrylic paints
Stencils

To reproduce the photo-graphed project, use the DecoArt Americana paints listed below, or substitute them with other acrylic paints for a different look.

Light Buttermilk (DA164)—
2 bottles
Celery Green (DA208)
Country Blue (DA41)
Payne's Grey (DA167)
White (DA01)
Hauser Light Green (DA131)
Evergreen (DA82)
Asphaltum (DA180)
Black (DA67)
Cadmium Yellow (DA10)
Yellow Light (DA144)
Cadmium Orange (DA14)

If you'd like to reproduce this project exactly as it's shown, use the Stencilled Garden stencils listed here; they're available at specialty stencil stores and through mail-order suppliers. (See "Suppliers" on page 95.) For a different look, just substitute them with other stencils.

Blueberry Vine (TSG406)
Winged Wonders (TSG702)

Instructions

1. Your butterfly house may come with a wooden post and assembly instructions. If it doesn't, ask a woodworker to make a post and adapt the butterfly house to fit it. (See step 8 of this section and "Wood—and a Friendly Woodworker" on page 14.)

2. Prepare the wooden butterfly house and wooden post for painting. (See "Preparing Wood" on pages 16–17.)

3. The base coat on the walls of the butterfly house is Light Buttermilk, and the base coat on the roof of the house and on the wooden post is Celery Green. Apply as many coats of paint as necessary to achieve smooth, opaque coverage. (See "Base-Coat Painting" on page 18.)

4. Stencil the designs. For correct design and color placement, refer to the project photos and to the "Stencil Color Guide" provided below. For detailed stenciling instructions, see "Stenciling" on pages 18–20.

5. To create an antique finish on the roof, first apply a coat of varnish to it. Allow the varnish to dry completely.

6. Use a 2" or 3" chip brush to apply the gel stain to the varnished roof. (The applied color should be uneven and streaky in appearance.) While the gel stain is still wet, use a rag to wipe it. Allow the gel stain to dry completely. (See "Antique Finishes" on pages 21–22.)

7. Sign your butterfly house and allow all the paint to dry for several days. Then protect your work by applying at least 3 coats of exterior varnish. (See "Final Touches" on page 23.)

8. Attach the wooden post to the butterfly house, or ask a woodworker to do this for you.

Stencil Color Guide

Blueberry Vine

Country Blue, Payne's Grey, White,
Hauser Light Green, Evergreen, Asphaltum

Winged Wonders

Black, White, Cadmium Yellow, Yellow Light, Cadmium Orange

"Fresh Cherries" Paper-Towel Holder

Combine bold checks with dainty dots, flowers, and cherries to make a darling container for paper towels.

Tools and Supplies

See pages 9–14 for more details on tools and supplies.

- 1 birdhouse-style paper-towel holder
- 4 wooden ball knobs, 1³⁄₄" diameter
- 1 metal door faceplate with screws
- 1 decorative glass doorknob with screw
- Screwdriver
- Electric drill
- Drill bit to match doorknob screw
- Embossing tool
- A friendly woodworker
- E6000 adhesive
- Acrylic paints
- Stencils

To reproduce the photographed project, use the DecoArt Americana paints listed below, or substitute them with other acrylic paints for a different look.

White (DA01)
French Vanilla (DA184)
Santa Red (DA170)
Napa Red (DA165)
Hauser Light Green (DA131)
Evergreen (DA82)
Country Blue (DA41)
Black (DA67)

If you'd like to reproduce this project exactly as it's shown, use the Stencilled Garden stencils listed here; they're available at specialty stencil stores and through mail-order suppliers. (See "Suppliers" on page 95.) For a different look, just substitute them with other stencils.

Fresh Cherries (TSG223)
Checkerboards (TSG706)

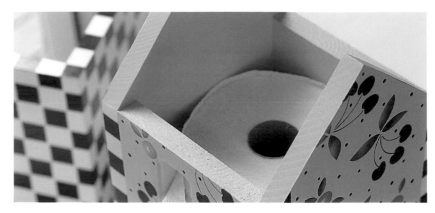

Instructions

1. Prepare the wooden paper towel holder, wooden ball knobs, and metal door faceplate for painting. (See "Preparing Wood" on pages 16–17 and "Preparing Metal" on page 15.)

2. The base coat on the roof is White, the base coat on the walls is French Vanilla, the base coat on the faceplate is Santa Red, and the base coat on the wooden ball knobs is Black. Apply as many coats of paint as necessary to achieve smooth, opaque coverage. (See "Base-Coat Painting" on page 18.)

3. Stencil the designs. For correct design and color placement, refer to the project photos. For detailed stenciling instructions, see "Stenciling" on pages 18–20.

4. Using an embossing tool, apply French Vanilla La De Da Dots to the flower centers, White La De Da Dots to the wooden ball knobs and to the door faceplate, and Black La De Da Dots randomly all over the paper-towel holder. (See "La De Da Dots" on pages 22–23.) For correct placement, refer to the project photos.

5. Sign your paper-towel holder and allow all the paint to dry for several days. Then protect your work by applying at least 3 coats of varnish. (See "Final Touches" on page 23.)

6. Attach the door faceplate to the paper-towel holder, using a screwdriver and the screws that came with the faceplate.

7. Before attaching the doorknob, you must predrill a hole for the screw. Position this hole in the wooden wall directly behind the hole in the faceplate. (If you like, ask a woodworker to do this for you.)

8. Position the doorknob in the hole of the faceplate, and attach it by driving the screw through the drilled hole in the wall.

9. Using E6000 adhesive, attach the wooden ball knobs to the bottom of the paper-towel holder.

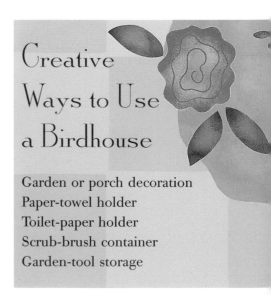

Creative Ways to Use a Birdhouse

Garden or porch decoration
Paper-towel holder
Toilet-paper holder
Scrub-brush container
Garden-tool storage

"Fruit on the Vine" Utensil Holder

Decorative drawer pulls support this fruit-patterned utensil holder.

Tools and Supplies

See pages 9–14 for more details on tools and supplies.

6" x 6" x 7" wooden box

Embossing tool

E6000 adhesive

4 decorative drawer pulls

Marbles or dry beans

Acrylic paints

Stencils

To reproduce the photographed project, use the DecoArt Americana paints listed below, or substitute them with other acrylic paints for a different look.

Sand (DA04)

Yellow Ochre (DA08)

Taffy Cream (DA05)

Jade Green (DA57)

Plantation Pine (DA113)

Asphaltum (DA180)

Shale Green (DA152)

Tomato Red (DA169)

Easy Blend Charcoal Grey (DEB28)

Cadmium Orange (DA14)

Georgia Clay (DA17)

Yellow Light (DA144)

Yellow Green (DA134)

Plum (DA175)

Black Plum (DA172)

If you'd like to reproduce this project exactly as it's shown, use the Stencilled Garden stencils listed here; they're available at specialty stencil stores and through mail-order suppliers. (See "Suppliers" on page 95.) For a different look, just substitute them with other stencils.

Diamond Vines (TSG242)

Apple (TSG421)

Orange (TSG419)

Lemon (TSG418)

Plum (TSG416)

Little Checks (TSG707)

Instructions

1. Prepare the wooden box for painting. (See "Preparing Wood" on pages 16–17.)

2. Apply as many coats of Sand paint as necessary to achieve smooth, opaque coverage on the entire box, inside and out. (See "Base-Coat Painting" on page 18.)

3. Stencil the designs. For correct design and color placement, refer to the project photos and to the "Stencil Color Guide" provided at right. For detailed stenciling instructions, see "Stenciling" on pages 18–20. *Here's a tip:* First, stencil the Diamond Vines stencil on all 4 sides of the box. Then layer the individual fruit designs over the vine designs, using a different fruit stencil on each side of the box.

4. Using an embossing tool, apply Yellow Ochre La De Da Dots to the flower centers. (See "La De Da Dots" on pages 22–23.)

5. Sign your utensil holder and allow all the paint to dry for several days. Then protect your work by applying at least 3 coats of varnish. (See "Final Touches" on page 23.)

6. Using E6000 adhesive, attach the decorative drawer pulls to the bottom of the utensil holder.

7. Fill one-third of the holder with marbles or dry beans, then push the handles of your utensils down into them. The weight of the beans or marbles will prevent the holder from tipping over.

Stencil Color Guide

Diamond Vines

Yellow Ochre

Apple

Taffy Cream, Jade Green, Plantation Pine, Asphaltum, Shale Green, Tomato Red, Easy Blend Charcoal Grey

Orange

Taffy Cream, Cadmium Orange, Georgia Clay, Jade Green, Plantation Pine, Asphaltum, Shale Green, Easy Blend Charcoal Grey

Lemon

Yellow Light, Yellow Green, Jade Green, Plantation Pine, Asphaltum, Shale Green, Easy Blend Charcoal Grey

Plum

Taffy Cream, Plum, Black Plum, Jade Green, Plantation Pine, Asphaltum, Shale Green, Easy Blend Charcoal Grey

¼" Checks from Little Checks

Yellow Ochre

Variation:
"Look to the Stars" Tissue Box

Let the night sky inspire you to turn a simple wooden box into a celestial tissue box. To make this tissue box, follow the instructions for the "Fruit on the Vine" utensil holder on pages 75-76 but substitute the tools and supplies with the ones listed at right. HERE'S A TIP: Stencil the "Gingham" design first on all four sides, and then layer the "Celestial" design over it.

Tools and Supplies

See pages 9–14 for more details on tools and supplies.

    6" x 6" x 7" wooden box
    Embossing tool
    4 star-shaped decorative
       knobs
    E6000 adhesive
    Acrylic paints
    Stencils

To reproduce the photographed project, use the DecoArt Americana paints listed below, or substitute them with other acrylic paints for a different look.

    Buttermilk (DA03)
    Sand (DA04)
    Moon Yellow (DA07)
    Admiral Blue (DA213)
    Marigold (DA194)

If you'd like to reproduce this project exactly as it's shown, use the Stencilled Garden stencils listed here; they're available at specialty stencil stores and through mail-order suppliers. (See "Suppliers" on page 95.) For a different look, just substitute them with other stencils.

    Celestial (TSG820)
    Gingham (TSG112S)

"Bee Americana" Lap Desk

Snazzy plaids and buzzing bees turn an ordinary wooden lap desk into a storage place for art materials, stationery, or photographs.

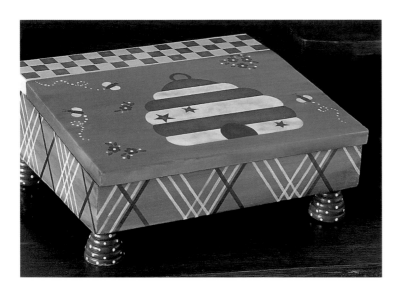

Tools and Supplies

See pages 9–14 for more details on tools and supplies.

- Wooden lap desk
- 4 turned wooden beehives, 1¾" diameter
- Embossing tool
- E6000 adhesive
- Acrylic paints
- Stencils

To reproduce the photographed project, use the DecoArt Americana paints listed below, or substitute them with other acrylic paints for a different look.

- Antique White (DA58)– 2 bottles
- Country Red (DA18)
- Admiral Blue (DA213)
- White Wash (DA02)
- Evergreen (DA82)

If you'd like to reproduce this project exactly as it's shown, use the Stencilled Garden stencils listed on page 79; they're available at specialty stencil stores and through mail-order suppliers. (See

"Suppliers" on page 95.) For a different look, just substitute them with other stencils.

    Buzzy Beeskep (TSG826)
    Wild Posies (TSG190)
    Scooter's Plaid (TSG124L)
    Checkerboards (TSG706)

Instructions

1. Prepare the wooden lap desk and turned wooden beehives for painting. (See "Preparing Wood" on pages 16–17.)

2. Apply as many coats of Antique White paint as necessary to achieve smooth, opaque coverage on the lap desk and beehives. (See "Base-Coat Painting" on page 18.)

3. The wooden beehives (these serve as feet for the lap desk) and the outer surface of the lid are color washed with Country Red. The body of the lap desk, both inside and outside, is color washed with Admiral Blue. Mix each of these washes and apply them with artist's brushes. (See "Color Washes" on page 21.)

4. Stencil the designs. For correct design and color placement, refer to the project photos and to the "Stencil Color Guide" provided at right. For detailed stenciling instructions, see "Stenciling" on pages 18–20.

5. Using an embossing tool, apply White Wash La De Da Dots to the flowers and turned wooden beehives, and use the same paint to create trails behind the bees. (See "La De Da Dots" on pages 22–23.) For correct placement, refer to the project photos.

6. Sign your lap desk and allow all the paint to dry for several days. Then protect your work by applying at least 3 coats of varnish. (See "Final Touches" on page 23.)

7. Using E6000 adhesive, attach the turned wooden beehives to the bottom of the lap desk.

Stencil Color Guide

Buzzy Beeskep

White Wash, Admiral Blue, Country Red

Flowers from Wild Posies

Admiral Blue, Evergreen

Scooter's Plaid

Admiral Blue, White Wash

¾" Checks from Checkerboards

Admiral Blue

"Whimsy Critters" Garden Ornaments

Use a jigsaw to turn scraps of wood into bright ornaments for your garden or flowerpots.

Tools and Supplies

See pages 9–14 for more details on tools and supplies.

A friendly woodworker

Jigsaw

2' length of untreated 1" x 6" lumber

Electric drill

¼" drill bit

3 metal rods, each ¼" x 3'

E6000 adhesive

Embossing tool

Scissors

Window-screen material, 18" square

Staple gun

Acrylic paints

Stencils

To reproduce the photographed projects, use the DecoArt Americana paints listed at right, or substitute them with other acrylic paints for a different look.

Moon Yellow (DA07)

Limeade (DA206)

Santa Red (DA170)

Black (DA67)

White (DA01)

Violet Haze (DA197)

If you'd like to reproduce these projects exactly as theiy're shown, use the Stencilled Garden stencils listed on page 81; they're available at specialty stencil stores and through mail-order suppliers. (See "Suppliers" on page 95.) For a different look, just substitute them with other stencils.

Curvy Checks (TSG715S)

Little Checks (TSG707)

Checkerboards (TSG706)

Squiggles & Dots (TSG178)

Instructions

1. Our wooden ladybug, bee, and dragonfly shapes were cut from a length of untreated pine, but any untreated wood will do. Use a jigsaw to cut the wood yourself, or sketch the critter shapes, using the project photo as a guide, and take them to a woodworker who can cut out the shapes for you. (See "Wood—and a Friendly Woodworker" on page 14.)

2. Drill a hole in one edge of each critter shape to accommodate the ¼"-diameter metal rod that will hold the critter upright, or ask a woodworker to do this for you.

3. Attach a metal rod to each critter shape by using E6000 adhesive to affix the rod inside the drilled hole. Allow the adhesive to dry.

4. Prepare each wooden critter shape for painting. (See "Preparing Wood" on pages 16–17.)

5. The base coats on the critters are as follows: Moon Yellow on the bee, Limeade on the dragonfly, and Santa Red on the ladybug. Apply as many coats of paint as necessary to achieve smooth, opaque coverage. (See "Base-Coat Painting" on page 18.)

6. Stencil the designs. For correct design and color placement, refer to the project photo and to the "Stencil Color Guide" provided below. For detailed stenciling instructions, see "Stenciling" on pages 18–20.

7. Using an artist's brush, hand paint White eyes on the ladybug and bee, and Black eyes on the dragonfly.

8. Using an embossing tool, apply Violet Haze La De Da Dots to the dragonfly, and Black La De Da Dots to the bee and ladybug.

9. Sign your critters and allow all the paint to dry for several days. Then protect your work by applying at least 3 coats of exterior varnish. (See "Final Touches" on page 23.) Make sure you use exterior varnish if you plan to set your critters outdoors.

10. Using scissors, cut 4 double-wing shapes from the window-screen material. Use a staple gun to attach 1 shape to the bee, 1 to the ladybug, and 2 to the dragonfly. Then bend the wings upward on both sides of the staples.

11. Set your critters in individual houseplants, or use them in your garden.

Stencil Color Guide

Curvy Checks

Black, White

¼" Checks from Little Checks

Black, White

¾" Checks from Checkerboards

Black, White

Squiggles from Squiggles & Dots

Black

Decorating Glass and Painting on Tile

As painters, we have a hard time leaving any surface untouched, but painting on glass was one of our greatest challenges. In fact, we tried just about every product for glass painting when we first started—and used to wonder if this process was ever meant to be.

We're stubborn individuals, however; we didn't give up. Several years ago, we took a class together to learn about new products and techniques from DecoArt and picked up a painting-on-tissue-paper technique that is similar to decoupage. We decided to try applying tissue paper to glass jars and then painting on the paper—and it worked!

Judy's main business is recycling old windows, and as we searched for new ways to treat the windows she found, we discovered a glass-etching product that we liked. We now use this product, Etchall Etching Creme, on a variety of glass surfaces, not just on window glass. It's easy to apply, and the effects are wonderful.

We also mastered the art of stenciling on tiles by playing around with our preparation techniques for other surfaces. We haven't figured out how to create painted tiles that are heat-resistant yet, but maybe that will come next. And until that time, our tiles are fun to make and are wonderful decorative items to enhance any room in your home.

"Wee Bee Buzzin'" Pencil Jar

Marbles or beans at the bottom of a painted canning jar lift pencils for easy retrieval.

Tools and Supplies

See pages 9–14 for more details on tools and supplies.

- 1-quart canning jar
- White tissue paper
- Faux glazing medium
- Acrylic paints
- Stencil

To reproduce the photographed project, use the DecoArt Americana paints listed below, or substitute them with other acrylic paints for a different look.

- Raw Sienna (DA93)
- Asphaltum (DA180)
- Marigold (DA194)
- Moon Yellow (DA07)
- Plantation Pine (DA113)
- Charcoal Grey (DA88)
- Soft Black (DA155)
- Black (DA67)
- Evergreen (DA82)

If you'd like to reproduce this project exactly as it's shown, use the Stencilled Garden stencil listed here; it's available at specialty stencil stores and through mail-order suppliers. (See "Suppliers" on page 95.) For a different look, just substitute them with another stencil.

Honey Pot (TSG193)

Instructions

1. Prepare the canning jar for painting. (See "Preparing Glass and Tile" on page 17.)
2. Tear the white tissue paper into small pieces. Affix these to the jar, one by one, by placing each piece against the jar's surface and applying faux glazing medium over it with an artist's brush. Make sure that each piece adheres completely to the jar, and overlap the pieces as you work. (This technique is very similar to decoupage.) Continue applying the tissue-paper pieces until the entire jar is covered up to the rim. Allow the tissue paper to dry completely.
3. Stencil the designs, using all the colors listed for this project except Evergreen. For correct design and color placement, refer to the project photos. For detailed stenciling instructions, see "Stenciling" on pages 18–20.
4. The ground area beneath the beehive is created with a ¼"-wide stencil brush and Evergreen paint. Start by off-loading some of the paint from your brush so that the brush is very dry. Then, holding the brush at an angle, apply the paint with a scrubbing motion, going back and forth over the areas where you want this color.
5. To create the grass blades on the jar, start by pouring a dime-sized pool of Evergreen paint onto your paint palette. Add a couple of drops of extender to the paint and enough water to make it the texture of light cream. Diluting the paint in this manner will help you achieve smooth, continuous brush strokes. To paint each blade of grass, use a long liner brush, holding it perpendicular to the jar's surface. Start at the bottom of the grass area and brush upward, lifting the brush up at the end of each stroke.
6. Sign your pencil jar and allow all the paint to dry for several days. Then protect your work by applying at least 3 coats of varnish. (See "Final Touches" on page 23.)

"Ladybug Fly Away" Bird Feeder

Top a chicken feeder with an ordinary canning jar to create a fanciful eating spot for birds.

Tools and Supplies

See pages 9–14 for more details on tools and supplies.

- 1-quart canning jar
- White tissue paper
- Faux glazing medium
- Metal chicken feeder (see "Accessories" on page 14)
- Scissors
- Miracle Sponge
- Embossing tool
- Acrylic paints
- Stencil

To reproduce the photographed project, use the DecoArt Americana paints listed below, or substitute them with other acrylic paints for a different look.

- Santa Red (DA170)
- Buttermilk (DA03)
- Black (DA67)
- Country Blue (DA41)
- Hauser Light Green (DA131)
- Evergreen (DA82)
- Moon Yellow (DA07)

If you'd like to reproduce this project exactly as it's shown, use the Stencilled Garden stencil listed here; it's available at specialty stencil stores and through mail-order suppliers. (See "Suppliers" on page 95.) For a different look, just substitute it with another stencil.

Lady Bug Border (TSG224)

Instructions

1. Prepare the canning jar and metal chicken feeder for painting. (See "Preparing Glass and Tile" on page 17 and "Preparing Metal" on page 15.)

2. Tear the white tissue paper into small pieces. Affix these to the jar, one by one, by placing each piece against the jar's surface and applying faux glazing medium over it with an artist's brush. Make sure that each piece adheres completely to the jar, and overlap the pieces as you work. (This technique is very similar to decoupage.) Continue applying the tissue-paper pieces until the entire jar is covered up to the rim. Allow the tissue paper to dry completely.

3. The base coat on the chicken feeder is Santa Red, and the base coat on the tissue-covered jar is Buttermilk. Apply as many coats of paint as necessary to achieve smooth, opaque coverage. (See "Base-Coat Painting" on page 18.)

4. Stencil the designs, using all the colors listed for this project except Buttermilk and Moon Yellow. For correct design and color placement, refer to the project photo. For detailed stenciling instructions, see "Stenciling" on pages 18–20.

5. To create the checks around the top and bottom of the jar, first use the scissors to cut a ½" square from the Miracle Sponge. Moisten the cut square with water and wait for it to grow. Then squeeze the excess water from it. Pour a small amount of Black paint onto your paint palette and dab the moist sponge into the paint. Using the project photo as a placement guide, press the sponge against the jar to create the checkerboard patterns.

6. Using an embossing tool, apply Moon Yellow La De Da Dots to the flower centers and Black La De Da Dots randomly around the flowers. (See "La De Da Dots" on pages 22–23.)

7. Sign your bird feeder and allow all the paint to dry for several days. Then protect your work by applying at least 3 coats of exterior varnish. (See "Final Touches" on page 23.)

8. To attach the chicken feeder, twist its threaded center onto the jar as if the feeder were a lid.

Creative Ways to Use a Canning Jar

Pencil holder
Utensil holder
Container for cotton balls
Container for dried goods
Tea-bag canister

Variation:
"Red, White, and Blue" Candy Feeder

Flashy stencils transform a canning jar and chicken feeder into a fun candy dispenser. To make this candy feeder, follow the instructions for the "Ladybug Fly Away" bird feeder on pages 85–86 but substitute the tools and supplies with the ones listed at right.

Tools and Supplies

See pages 9–14 for more details on tools and supplies.

- 1-quart canning jar
- White tissue paper
- Faux glazing medium
- Metal chicken feeder (see "Accessories" on page 14)
- Embossing tool
- Acrylic paints
- Stencil

To reproduce the photographed project, use the DecoArt Americana paints listed below, or substitute them with other acrylic paints for a different look.

- White (DA01)
- Tomato Red (DA169)
- Admiral Blue (DA213)

If you'd like to reproduce this project exactly as it's shown, use the Stencilled Garden stencil listed here; it's available at specialty stencil stores and through mail-order suppliers. (See "Suppliers" on page 95.) For a different look, just substitute it with another stencil.

Let's Be A Star (TSG180)

"How Wild Can You Get?" Coasters

Pair bold animal patterns with pretty flowers to turn common tiles into customized coasters.

Tools and Supplies

See pages 9–14 for more details on tools and supplies.

    4 tiles, 4" square
    Large, empty bottle with lid
    Embossing tool
    16 self-adhesive surface
        guards, 3/8" diameter
    Acrylic paints
    Stencils

To reproduce the photographed project, use the DecoArt Americana paints listed below, or substitute them with other acrylic paints for a different look.

    Violet Haze (DA197)
    White (DA01)
    Reindeer Moss Green
        (DA187)
    Black (DA67)
    Plantation Pine (DA113)
    Buttermilk (DA03)

If you'd like to reproduce this project exactly as it's shown, use the Stencilled Garden stencils listed here; they're available at specialty stencil stores and through mail-order suppliers. (See "Suppliers" on page 95.) For a different look, just substitute them with other stencils.

    Zebra Print (TSG129)
    Giraffe Print (TSG230)
    Wild Animal Print (TSG128)
    Animal Print (TSG127)
    Ashley's Tea Party (TSG183)

Instructions

1. Prepare the tiles for painting. (See "Preparing Glass and Tile" on page 17.)
2. The base-coat color on the tiles is a mixture of Violet Haze and White. Pour the bottle of White paint into the large, empty bottle. Then add the bottle of Violet Haze paint and shake the fifty-fifty mixture well to create a pale violet color. (When dry, acrylic colors are darker than they appear in their bottles. To test a color, brush some of the

paint onto a piece of paper and let it dry.)

3. Apply as many coats of the pale violet paint as necessary to achieve smooth, opaque coverage on the entire surface of each tile. (See "Base-Coat Painting" on page 18.)

4. One corner of each tile is also painted with Reindeer Moss Green. Don't try to paint these corners freehand. Instead, position a piece of removable painter's tape diagonally across each tile to define a triangle at one corner. Burnish the tape edges well, then apply as many coats of Reindeer Moss Green as necessary to achieve smooth, opaque coverage on the tape-marked corner. Allow the paint to dry before removing the tape.

5. Stencil the designs. For correct design and color placement, refer to the project photo and to the "Stencil Color Guide" provided at right. For detailed stenciling instructions, see "Stenciling" on pages 18–20. *Here's a tip:* Before stenciling the tiles, apply tape along one side of the line between the two base-coated sections on each one. Stencil the exposed sections, and when the paint is dry, remove the tape. Then apply tape to the other side of the line on each tile and stencil the remaining sections.

6. Using an embossing tool, apply Black La De Da Dots randomly around the flowers and along the line that separates the two base-coat colors on each tile. Apply Buttermilk La De Da Dots to the flower centers. (See "La De Da Dots" on pages 22–23.) For correct placement, refer to the project photo.

7. Sign your tile coasters and allow all the paint to dry for several days. Then protect your work from "sweating" glasses and spills by applying at least 3 coats of exterior varnish. (See "Final Touches" on page 23.)

8. To prevent the coasters from scratching the surfaces on which you place them, attach 4 surface guards to the back corners of each one.

Stencil Color Guide

Zebra Print
Black

Giraffe Print
Black

Wild Animal Print
Black

Animal Print
Violet Haze, Black

Flowers from Ashley's Tea Party
Violet Haze, Plantation Pine

Variation:

"Girly Flowers and Gingham" Trivet

Decorative drawer pulls add height to this tile trivet, making it perfect for a spoon rest or condiment holder. To make this trivet, follow the instructions for the "How Wild Can You Get?" coasters on pages 88-89 but substitute the tools and supplies with the ones listed at right. HERE'S A TIP: First stencil the "Gingham" design, and then stencil the "Girly's Flowers" design over it.

Tools and Supplies

See pages 9–14 for more details on tools and supplies.

- Tile, 6" square
- Embossing tool
- E6000 adhesive
- 4 decorative drawer pulls
- Acrylic paints
- Stencils

To reproduce the photographed project, use the DecoArt Americana paints listed below, or substitute them with other acrylic paints for a different look.

- Buttermilk (DA03)
- Yellow Ochre (DA08)
- Hauser Light Green (DA131)
- Evergreen (DA82)
- Antique Mauve (DA162)
- Cranberry Wine (DA112)
- Black (DA67)

If you'd like to reproduce this project exactly as it's shown, use the Stencilled Garden stencils listed here; they're available at specialty stencil stores and through mail-order suppliers. (See "Suppliers" on page 95.) For a different look, just substitute them with other stencils.

- Gingham (TSG112S)
- Girly's Flowers (TSG175)

Variation:
"Cherries and Checks" Trivet

To make this trivet, follow the instructions for the "How Wild Can You Get?" coasters on pages 88–89 but substitute the tools and supplies with the ones listed at right. HERE'S A TIP: First stencil the black checkerboard pattern from "Fresh Cherries." Next, white out the black areas that will be covered by the cherry designs. (See "Whiting Out" on page 20.) Then stencil the cherry designs.

Tools and Supplies

See pages 9–14 for more details on tools and supplies.

> 8" tile, with angled corners
> 4 wooden ball knobs,
>   1 ½" diameter
> Embossing tool
> E6000 adhesive
> Acrylic paints
> Stencil

To reproduce the photographed project, use the DecoArt Americana paints listed below, or substitute them with other acrylic paints for a different look.

> Light Buttermilk (DA164)
> Black (DA67)
> Santa Red (DA170)
> Hauser Light Green (DA131)
> Evergreen (DA82)
> Moon Yellow (DA07)

If you'd like to reproduce this project exactly as it's shown, use the Stencilled Garden stencil listed here; it's available at specialty stencil stores and through mail-order suppliers. (See "Suppliers" on page 95.) For a different look, just substitute it with another stencil.

> Fresh Cherries (TSG223)

"Fergie's Birdhouse Collection" Tile

With paint and stencils, you can turn any tile into a delightful wall ornament.

Tools and Supplies

See pages 9–14 for more details on tools and supplies.

Tile, 10" square, with angled corners

Embossing tool

Plate hanger

Acrylic paints

Stencils

To reproduce the photographed project, use the DecoArt Americana paints listed below, or substitute them with other acrylic paints for a different look.

Sand (DA04)

White (DA01)

Black (DA67)

Moon Yellow (DA07)

Country Blue (DA41)

Hauser Light Green (DA131)

Evergreen (DA82)

Olive Green (DA56)

Royal Purple (DA150)

Tomato Red (DA169)

Winter Blue (DA190)

Williamsburg Blue (DA40)

Antique Gold (DA09)

Summer Lilac (DA189)

Pansy Lavender (DA154)

Easy Blend Charcoal Grey (DEB28)

If you'd like to reproduce this project exactly as it's shown, use the Stencilled Garden stencils listed here; they're available at specialty stencil stores and through mail-order suppliers. (See "Suppliers" on page 95.) For a different look, just substitute them with other stencils.

Fergie's Birdhouse Collection
  (TSG107)

Fergie's Accent Package
  (TSG108)

Instructions

1. Prepare the tile for painting. (See "Preparing Glass and Tile" on page 17.)
2. Apply as many Sand base coats to the tile as necessary to achieve smooth, opaque coverage. (See "Base-Coat Painting" on page 18.)
3. Stencil the designs. For correct design and color placement, refer to the project photo and to the "Stencil Color Guide" provided at right. For detailed stenciling instructions, see "Stenciling" on pages 18–20.
4. While the stencil is still in place, create the shadow effects on the picket fence by applying Easy Blend Charcoal Grey around the fence's edges.
5. Using an embossing tool, apply Olive Green La De Da Dots to the pole and roof of the middle birdhouse, and Country Blue La De Da Dots to the smallest birdhouse. (See "La De Da Dots" on pages 22–23.) For correct placement, refer to the project photos.
6. Sign your tile and allow all the paint to dry for several days. Then protect your work by applying at least 3 coats of varnish. (See "Final Touches" on page 23.)
7. Attach the plate hanger to the back of the tile, referring to the hanger manufacturer's instructions as necessary.

Creative
Ways to Use
a Tile

Coaster
Spoon rest
Trivet
Base for salt and
    pepper shakers
Welcome sign
Shelf or mantel ornament

Stencil Color Guide

Fergie's Birdhouse Collection

White, Black, Moon Yellow, Country Blue, Hauser Light Green, Evergreen, Olive Green, Royal Purple, Tomato Red

Fergie's Accent Package

Winter Blue, Williamsburg Blue, Antique Gold, Summer Lilac, Pansy Lavender, Hauser Light Green, Evergreen

"La De Da My Cherries" Window

Give an old window new life with splashy paint and elegant etching.

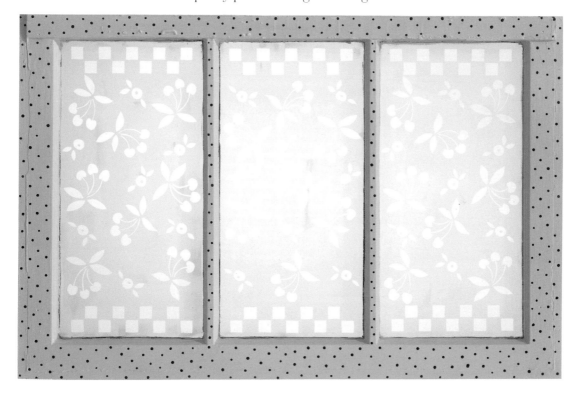

Tools and Supplies

See pages 9–14 for more details on tools and supplies.

- Three-pane window
- Embossing tool
- Con-Tact paper
- Pencil
- X-Acto blade
- Glass-etching medium
- Acrylic paints
- Stencil

To reproduce the photographed project, use the DecoArt Americana paints listed below, or substitute them with other acrylic paints for a different look.

> Moon Yellow (DA07)—
> 2 bottles
> Santa Red (DA170)

If you'd like to reproduce this project exactly as it's shown, use the Stencilled Garden stencil listed at top right; it's available at specialty stencil stores and through mail-order suppliers. (See "Suppliers" on page 95.) For a different look, just substitute it with another stencil.

> Fresh Cherries (TSG223)

Instructions

1. Prepare the wooden window frame for painting. (See "Preparing Wood" on pages 16–17.)
2. Apply as many Moon Yellow base coats to the

94

window frame as necessary to achieve smooth, opaque coverage. (See "Base-Coat Painting" on page 18.)

3. Using an embossing tool, apply Santa Red La De Da Dots to the window frame. (See "La De Da Dots" on pages 22–23.)

4. Sign your window frame and allow all the paint to dry for several days. Then protect your work by applying at least 3 coats of varnish to the wood. (See "Final Touches" on page 23.)

5. Clean the glass windowpanes and dry them with lint-free paper towels or a lint-free rag. (See "Preparing Glass and Tile" on page 17.)

6. Completely cover each glass pane with Con-Tact paper. Using the stencil and a pencil, trace the stencil designs onto the Con-Tact paper. Then expose the glass under the traced designs by cutting out the designs with an X-Acto blade.

7. Remove any bubbles under the Con-Tact paper by pressing the air out through the cut edges. To prevent the etching medium from creeping under the Con-Tact paper, burnish all the edges of the Con-Tact paper around the cut designs.

8. Referring to the manufacturer's instructions, etch the glass by applying the glass-etching medium to the exposed glass surfaces. (The Etchall Etching Creme we use is applied with a squeegee and left on the glass for 15 minutes. The creme can be scraped back into the bottle and reused.)

9. Remove all the Con-Tact paper under running water, rinsing away the etching medium at the same time. Wash and dry the glass.

10. Display your etched glass in a window or against a dark background. The etched designs will show up best if the glass is lit from behind or set off against a dark surface.

Suppliers

The Stencilled Garden
6029 North Palm Avenue
Fresno, CA 93704
(559) 449-1764
www.stencilledgarden.com
   Stencils, brushes, paints, faux-painting tools and supplies, AC's Acrylic Craft Paint Remover, brush cleaner/conditioner, brush scrubbers, unpainted projects, decorative accessories

DecoArt
PO Box 386
Stanford, KY 40484
(800) 367-3047
www.decoart.com
   Acrylic paints, glazes, gel stains

Eagle Brush Company, Inc.
431 Commerce Park Drive SE, Suites 100 & 101
Marietta, GA 30060
(800) 832-4532
   Art brushes

About the Authors

Judy Skinner   Jennifer Ferguson

An artist, designer, and teacher of the arts of stenciling and faux finishing, Jennifer Ferguson has been painting for the past thirteen years. Through her company, The Stencilled Garden, she designs stencils and teaches stenciling and faux finishing, and she sells stenciling and faux-finishing supplies at her shop. Jennifer has appeared many times on *The Carol Duvall Show* and has also appeared on *Aleene's Creative Living* and the *Kitty Bartholomew Show*, where she shared some of her ideas and projects with viewers. When she isn't attending trade shows or painting projects, Jennifer enjoys spending time with her family and working on their new home.

An artist, "house stripper," and recycler, Judy Skinner has been creating art for more than twenty years. Through her own company, Collectiques by JuBee, she recycles old windows, doors, drawers, and any other house parts she can find by transforming them into works of art that she sells at art shows throughout California and Nevada. When she isn't attending art shows or finding houses to strip, Judy enjoys spending time with her family and finishing projects for their home.

Jennifer and Judy met at Jennifer's shop back in 1996, and since then, they've developed a wonderful friendship. Their mutual love for the arts of recycling, painting, stenciling, and faux finishing gives them much to share. They travel all over the United States to attend conventions, and they have taken these great opportunities to indulge in "junking" trips and to find many treasures. *Painted Whimsies* is the second book for this duo; *Painted Chairs* was their first, and they're planning many more. They both hope that you will enjoy this book and that you will fall in love with painting as they have.